Harrow
A to Z

DON WALTER

SUTTON PUBLISHING

First published in 2005 by
Sutton Publishing Limited · Phoenix Mill
Thrupp · Stroud · Gloucestershire · GL5 2BU

British Library Cataloguing in Publication Data
A catalogue record for this book is available from the British Library.

ISBN 0-7509-3985-0

Title page photograph: Mid-nineteenth-century view of Harrow School and the parish
church of St Mary's, still Harrow's best-loved buildings.

This one is for my fellow writers
Sheena Crawley and Christian Duffin

Typeset in 11/14.25 pt Galliard.
Typesetting and origination by
Sutton Publishing Limited.
Printed and bound in England by
J.H. Haynes & Co. Ltd, Sparkford.

INTRODUCTION

As even the quickest glance at its contents will reveal, this book is most definitely not an A to Z of Harrow history in the way that a geographical gazetteer comprehensively lists every city, town and village. Rather it is a collection of 26 pieces about certain aspects of our town's rich and colourful past.

That these pieces are presented alphabetically rather than chronologically stems from the fact that they began life as a somewhat unusual – but, in the event, highly popular – series of articles in Harrow's local paper, the *Harrow Observer*. At the time of their publication, many readers commented that they would happily read more about the series' varied topics so, for this edition, every piece has been considerably extended – and, as you can see, fully illustrated from my own (and the borough's) photographic archives.

Each piece should be of interest in itself. Nevertheless, if read together, they will also provide an intriguing, if inevitably selective, portrait of Harrow life over a number of centuries.

Harrow's history is, of course, a good deal longer than the events recorded here. Our parish church of St Mary's, Harrow on the Hill, for example, was founded as early as 1087, and there is ample evidence that it was preceded by a Saxon church on the same site where, almost certainly, pagan rites were performed in even earlier times.

By the appearance in about 1086 of Domesday Book, William the Conqueror's amazing record of the lands he had conquered, the Hill was already a sizeable community. Although only one of countless manors in the land, Harrow may well have held a special significance for the Norman king in that the Lordship of the Manor was then held by Archbishop Lanfranc, who was not only the monarch's Archbishop of Canterbury but also a close personal friend. (Subsequent archbishops, in fact, were to retain the Harrow Manor right up to the reign of King Henry VIII.)

According to Domesday, there were at least 117 people living on the archbishop's manor, including a priest, three knights, seven vassals (the knight's tenants), 102 villeins (who owed service to the lord), two cottagers and two serfs. There may even have been an early Flambard among them for, as is revealed later in the book, the name is one of the very oldest in our history.

One mystery remains – in these early years where did the archbishop himself reside when holding court within his manor? After all, Headstone Manor, which is known to have been built for the archbishops, was not actually completed until about 1340. Informed opinion now favours a residence somewhere in the Sudbury area but, in reality, no site has ever been established beyond shadow of doubt.

Although the subject is not covered in this particular volume, it is nevertheless worth recalling that King Henry III granted an annual fair and a weekly market to Harrow as early as 1261. Both these activities were held on the open ground we now call the Church Fields and, because they attracted the occasional unscrupulous trader and light-fingered customer, it was found necessary to build a court-house on adjoining land. Amazingly enough, this building still remains – in an alleyway off West Street leading to the Fields. It is, however, virtually unknown to the majority of local residents because for decades it has formed part of a local plastics company. Possibly, too, it origins have been obscured by the name by which it was known for centuries, the

The Pye House, off West Street, from an engraving dated 1795.

Pye House. Though this suggests some sort of bake-house, the name is actually a corruption of the Norman French 'pieds poudreux', which roughly translates as dusty-footed – an apt enough description of those who made the journey to the markets over what can only have been the crudest of tracks.

Given that experts have dated what remains of the court-house to around 1350, the Pye House may well challenge Headstone Manor for the title of the borough's second oldest surviving building.

By comparison, the present Harrow School, whose origins are recalled in our first chapter, is a relative newcomer. I write the 'present' Harrow School quite deliberately for late nineteenth-century researches have conclusively established that John Lyon, once credited as the school's founder, is far more likely to have re-founded an existing school by endowing it with revenues from some of the many acres he owned both locally and in London.

Scholars can still only guess exactly when this earlier school was started, but a Court Roll of Harrow Manor dated May 1475 makes reference to a school 'inside the churchyard' while, almost one hundred years earlier, another manorial record states that one John Intowne was punished because 'he delivered his son William into remote parts to learn the Liberal Arts', which seems to suggest that young William could have acquired such knowledge on home ground! In the event, today's 'original' school building – the left-hand wing of the so-called Old Schools – dates from only 1615, some years after the death of both John Lyon and his widow, Joan.

If the original Old Schools may not be quite as old as some imagine, it has thankfully survived, which is more than can be said of Canons. As recorded here, this was one of the greatest mansions ever built – not just in our locality but anywhere in Britain – yet it was pulled down within a quarter of a century of its creation. Fortunately for us, the Duke of Chandos, who poured a fortune into Canons, had money to spare for the rebuilding of the church of St Lawrence, Whitchurch. In the early twenty-first century, this is still much visited both for its glorious baroque decoration and for its intimate connection with the great composer George Frideric Handel who, as the Duke's Music Master, regularly played the organ that still survives in the church.

Handel, of course, is only one of a gallery of exciting personalities who have links with Harrow and many of their stories are told in the following pages – from the eighteenth-century miser Daniel Dancer through to such fascinating Victorians as the early feminist Annie Besant, Sir William Gilbert of Gilbert and Sullivan fame, novelist Anthony Trollope and his indomitable mother Fanny and the sad Horatia Nelson, who spent a lifetime hiding the fact that she was the illegitimate child of Lord Nelson by his liaison with Emma Hamilton.

A familiar king, a less familiar queen and a trio of prime ministers also figure in our narrative which, as it moves into the twentieth century, chronicles the birth and growth of local industries (Kodak among them) and social institutions such as the Salvation Army. You will find, too, a backward glance at the subject of health care (see pp. 37–42) in a borough which still includes Hygeia, the Goddess of Health, in its coat of arms.

Even though a complete book could and perhaps should be written about our town's involvement in two world wars, this A to Z must be content with a few fascinating facts about Zeppelins and a reminder of the now-forgotten lady who was among the first women to win an OBE, for recruiting women to the country's munition factories during the First World War.

In contrast, our chapters on the years between the wars are suitably light-hearted, concentrating on the entertainment provided by stars such as Jessie Matthews and the cinemas that showed her films including one picture palace – the former Harrow Granada – which she opened at the height of her fame. Nor have I totally neglected the more recent past, as witness the story of our very new University of Westminster, which is also featured.

Once home to the Archbishop of Canterbury, Headstone Manor was a working farm between the two world wars.

As I wrote earlier, this book started life as a series of newspaper articles. It is, therefore, entirely appropriate that, in recreating the past century and a half, I have been heavily reliant on reports (and, indeed, illustrations) first published in the *Harrow Observer* and its predecessor, the *Harrow Gazette*. Since the latter first appeared as long ago as 1855, it is, in itself, part of Harrow's history.

As with my seven previous volumes, I have also had the privilege of free and unfettered use of that treasure-house of memories, the Harrow Local History Collection, especially its unique photographic archive.

From this brief introduction alone, readers will have realised that Harrow has been home to so many major personalities and events that virtually every letter in the alphabet could have embraced at least half a dozen alternatives: Archbishop Anselm, poet Matthew Arnold, politician Clement Attlee, Byron's ill-fated daughter Allegra; Byron himself and Thomas Becket; Winston Churchill and Anthony Ashley Cooper (better known as the philanthropist Lord Shaftesbury) are just a few of those clamouring for our attention at the very beginning of the alphabet.

So if you have found something of interest and amusement in this very first A to Z, remember, there could indeed be another . . . always supposing I can bend my mind to the little problem of the alternative Xs and Zs!

Archery

A Silver Arrow
contestant in the
costume specially
created for the event.

Hard as it may be to believe, archery once meant far more to the citizens of Harrow than, say, football does today for – in Tudor times, and earlier – it was regarded as a means of defence as much as a sporting activity. No wonder then that in 1559, one year after Queen Elizabeth I came to the throne, the Harrow Manorial Court actually issued an order that every male over the age of 12 should possess a bow and arrow.

It was against this background that in 1579 John Lyon, the founder (some say re-founder) of Harrow School ordained in his written statutes for the conduct of the school that all pupils should be provided with 'a bow, three shafts, bow-strings and a bracer'.

So far, so ordinary perhaps – until in 1648 a Harrow Hill resident, former diplomat Sir Gilbert Talbot, came up with an idea that was to transform a fairly commonplace activity into something infinitely grander and more exciting. This he achieved by presenting the school with a silver arrow to be shot for annually by up to 12 scholars. The ensuing Silver Arrow Contest became so popular that the governors were soon obliged to provide new archery butts on the hill side of what is now called Roxeth Hill. Significantly enough, in Edwardian times, there was a house called The Butts just across the way from the spot where we believe the butts to have been. Only a matter of yards away in London Road was – indeed, still is – Tollgate Cottage, almost certainly the home of the man who held the very special title of Keeper of the Butts.

Surviving descriptions of the butts refer to a highly picturesque spot, crowned with majestic trees, and with grassy seats actually cut in terraces into the hillside. According to a 1731 newspaper report, about a thousand people could be accommodated.

Thomas Thackeray, Harrow School headmaster from 1749 to 1760, had such a high regard for the event that he even added two crossed arrows to the original school badge of a lion rampant (obviously a visual pun on the name of the founder).

Nor was its importance lost on the schoolboy Richard Brinsley Sheridan, whose feckless father provided barely enough money for his fees let alone

Playwright Richard Brinsley Sheridan, who needed new clothes for the contest.

his clothing. In 1776, in a touching letter now housed in the school archives, the playwright-to-be wrote to an uncle: 'The course of my present letter is partly my want of clothes for my brown ones are quite gone . . . and those which I have now, being of a very light colour and having met with a few accidents, are not remarkably clean.' Happily, the uncle saw that he received new garments in ample time for the Silver Arrow Contest which, by the time of Sheridan's schooldays, had acquired more and more in the way of colourful detail.

The contestants were now elaborately clad in spangled green and white satin; good shots were acclaimed by a concert of French horns, and the ultimate winner was carried back in triumph to the school where that night he was expected to give – at his own expense – a spectacular ball in the school's Dancing Hall.

Illustrated scorecard produced for the 1769 contest.

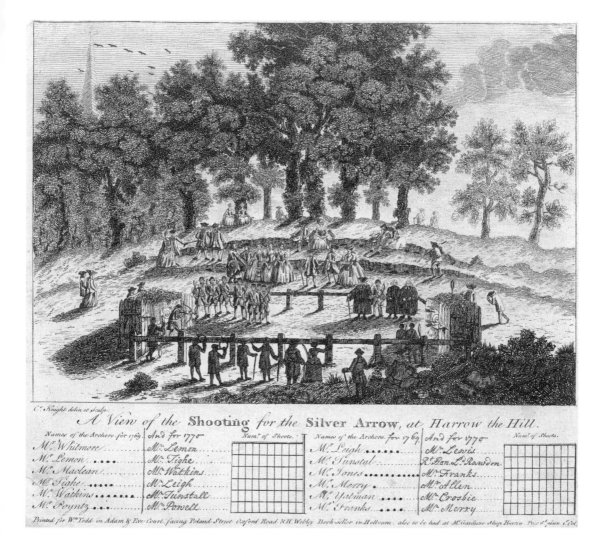

A View of the Shooting for the Silver Arrow, at Harrow the Hill.

Head boy John Sawyer painted in costume by George Romney, *c.* 1770.

Visitors regularly came from distant parts; even, in 1765, a Red Indian chieftain who, though complimentary about the boys' skills, claimed that he could have outshot the lot! Then, in 1771, when the arrow was won by Lord Althorp, afterwards the 2nd Earl Spencer, some kind of accident occurred. Tradition has it that a spectator – some reports identify the town barber – was hit in the face with an arrow. But whatever actually happened, it was enough to prompt the new headmaster, Benjamin Heath, to cancel the 1772 event and to substitute the infinitely more serious programme now known as Speech Day.

This accident was probably the excuse Heath had been waiting for, not least because the competitors' insistence on lengthy practice time was seriously interfering with their studies. The event was also thought to be bringing crowds of undesirables to the town. His action, however, did nothing to improve his relationship with the school, already soured by the fact that he was (perish the thought!) an Old Etonian and had been appointed in preference to Samuel Parr, a true Harrovian in that he had been both Head of School as a boy and a favourite assistant master as a man.

Eventually, the school's resentment erupted into violence. As Thomas Grimston wrote home at the time: 'We carried our resentment as far as we thought necessary which I'm afraid you will think a good deal too far . . . having first locked the School up, (we) ran down to the public inn and drew out Mr. Bucknall's chaise – one of the Governors who called us blackguards. We drew it out of Harrow town, hollowing all the time and knocking it to pieces with our bludgeons.'

One of the ringleaders of this surprising revolt was the 11-year-old Richard Wellesley, whose family thought it politic to remove him to Eton. He was duly followed there by his younger brother, Arthur, later to become the great Duke of Wellington. Thus, a moment of juvenile

Late eighteenth-century engraving of schoolboys practising archery on the Church Fields.

An early game of cricket at Harrow, 1772. Note the curved bat and spindly stumps.

bravado robbed Harrow not only of a future prime minister but also of the opportunity of claiming in later years that it was on the playing fields of Harrow – not of Eton – that the Battle of Waterloo had been won!

For all that further accounts of the contest appeared in the London papers (such as the *Morning Herald* of 1816), it can safely be assumed that these were false stories deliberately 'planted' by mischievous boys and, in truth, the Silver Arrow totally disappeared from the Harrow scene for over two centuries.

The memory, however, lived on and, in 1910, C.J. Maltby and Percy Buck were inspired to write a rousing addition to the official school song book. Entitled 'The Silver Arrow', its verses urged the youth of the day:

> 'to rise in your strength and show
> by word and deed
> you are worthy seed
> of your sires who drew the bow'

Despite this exhortation, it took a further 214 years (until 1986) for the contest to re-emerge, albeit in a somewhat different guise. On this occasion, the prime mover was the then Mayor of Harrow, Peter Pitt, who reintroduced a contest which not only involved both pupils of Harrow School and the John Lyon School but was also open to experienced Middlesex archers. Although a considerable success on its debut, this new Silver Arrow, unlike its illustrious predecessor, has yet to establish itself as an annual event in the Harrow calendar.

Annie Besant

The nineteenth-century social reformer whose remarkable journey began at Harrow Hill's vicarage.

It has long been matter for surprise that Annie Besant is not more widely known, for her life impacted on more people and more worthwhile causes than almost any other nineteenth-century woman I can name. In a crowded 85 years, she championed the strike of London's match girls, survived a prosecution for obscenity (losing custody of a child in the process), introduced free meals for needy children and was one of the true pioneers of Indian Home Rule.

Annie Besant was not actually born in Harrow (the City of London can claim that honour) and her arrival in our midst was almost entirely due to the fact that one of Harrow's most charismatic vicars, the Revd John Cunningham, chose not to live at St Mary's vicarage, hard-by Harrow School at the top of Church Hill. Instead, he took a lease on the large house originally built by Thomas Trollope on Julian Hill (see p. 94), leaving the vicarage empty, a fact which Annie's penurious widowed mother, Mrs Wood, was quick to see as a money-making opportunity.

Three years earlier, Mrs Wood had lost her husband in highly unusual circumstances. A city businessman at the time of his death, he had actually trained as a doctor but had never practised. Neverthless, having maintained some of his old medical friendships, he was occasionally allowed to assist at interesting dissections. On one such occasion he cut his finger on the breastbone of a victim of consumption. The wound never healed and, all too quickly, he died of what we would now call tuberculosis.

Like so many other widows before and after her (Mary Shelley is a prime example), Mrs Wood now sought some less expensive way of giving Annie's brother a public school education. Realising that Harrow School was blessed with more boarders than houses in which to accommodate them, Mrs Wood approached the headmaster, Charles Vaughan (see p. 103), with the idea that she should run the empty vicarage as a kind of Dame's House caring for a limited number of Harrow pupils. With the proviso that a male house tutor should live under the same roof, Vaughan agreed.

Annie was then a highly impressionable eight-year-old and was greatly taken with the charming old vicarage and especially its garden. Years later, in her autobiography, she was to write lovingly of a trapdoor in its back fence which, she said, swung open to reveal one of the fairest views in England (undoubtedly that towards Windsor that can still be enjoyed from St Mary's Terrace).

Annie became an accomplished pianist and therefore performed frequently at the musical evenings, which were then an established feature of the Hill's social scene. On one such occasion she seems to

have met Miss Ellen Marryat, sister of the author Captain Marryat (whose adventure stories such as *Children of the New Forest* still occasionally grace our television screens). Much taken with Annie, Miss Marryat invited her to become a companion to her niece, which necessitated a partial move from Harrow to Dorset.

Annie Besant (centre) seen with the Match Girls' Strike Committee, in 1888. *(Tower Hamlets Local History Library)*

This was to prove the first of many momentous journeys for Annie. Married at 20 to a clergyman Frank Besant, who was somewhat older than herself, she later became professionally involved with a self-proclaimed atheist, Charles Bradlaugh, with whom she founded the Free Thought Publishing Company. In 1877, true to its name, the company brought out a pamphlet that dared to advocate birth control, and both Bradlaugh and Annie Besant were brought to trial accused of 'depraving public morals'. Found guilty of publishing 'an obscene libel', they were both sentenced to six months but, although this harsh judgment was later quashed by the Court of Appeal, a vindictive husband used the case to claim custody of their daughter.

Subsequently, it was left to Annie – and like-minded liberals including George Bernard Shaw – to champion the cause of the cruelly used women employees of the match company, Bryant & May, resulting in the unique Match Girls' Strike. Not only was the strike successful, for from it emerged the first-ever women's trade union. Later still, as a

St Mary's centuries-old vicarage where Annie spent a happy childhood.

member of the influential London School Board, Annie was largely instrumental in securing free lunches and medical treatment for needy pupils of the capital's elementary schools.

Becoming a convert to the Hindu-inspired doctrines of the Russian-born theosophist Helena Blavatsky, Annie Besant spent much of her later career promoting the cause of theosophy in both the USA and India. Ultimately, the politics of the latter country became her ruling passion. In 1916, she founded the Indian Home Rule League and, a year later, became the first chairman of the Indian National Congress.

Inevitably, her travels allowed her relatively few opportunities to return to Harrow although in November 1890 the *Harrow Gazette* reported a speech she gave on Socialism to the Harrow Liberal Club. It was, she said, a great pleasure to be back, 'for many of my happiest memories are associated with this place'.

Annie Besant died in Madras in 1933 – miles away from the place she once called home.

Canons

The excessive
lavishness of
Canons is mocked
in this 1731
cartoon.

Canons could have been as famous a survivor as Blenheim Palace. It was, after all, one of the grandest mansions England had ever known, boasting a domestic staff of nearly one hundred; moreover, its personal music master was none other than the great Mr Handel himself.

Yet today all that remains is a pair of entrance columns standing at the junction of Canons Drive and Edgware Road – and its name, subsequently bestowed upon the Canons Park estate and Canons Park station on the Jubilee Line.

Even when new, Canons was dogged by controversy. Its builder, James Brydges, later the Duke of Chandos, had been Paymaster General to the Army and was widely believed to have lined his pockets at the country's expense (although he escaped censure when the inevitable enquiry was held). In the event, his creation of Canons cost him something like a quarter of a million pounds, a truly awe-inspiring sum for the day.

For his money, he got a Palladian-style mansion with some ninety rooms, approached by four impressive avenues. That from Edgware was three-quarters of a mile long and had, at its entrance, lodgings for eight former sergeants of Marlborough's army whom Brydges employed as watchmen.

There were also 83 acres of walled gardens, including such features as a specially constructed canal fed from the Spring Pond on Stanmore's Little Common, a lake, fountains and a picturesque artificial mound known as Bellmount, in fact the forerunner of today's residential district of Belmont.

Nevertheless its considerable pretensions earned it much contemporary criticism, the satirist Alexander Pope even writing 'An Epitaph on False Taste', in which he mockingly declared 'His building is a town, his pond an ocean, his parterre, a down'.

Although the house had its own domestic chapel, Brydges also set about rebuilding the nearby church of St Lawrence, Whitchurch. Again, no expense was spared and, within a perhaps surprisingly modest exterior, the talents of noted European artists and craftsmen fashioned a monument to the baroque style that, to this day, is thought to be unique in England.

Then, as a crowning glory, in 1718 he appointed George Frideric Handel as his music master. The noted German-born though English-based composer remained at Canons some two years, during which time he produced many memorable works. Among them were the *Chandos Te Deum*, some eleven Chandos anthems and a masque which he later transformed into the familiar oratorio, *Esther*.

As his chaplain, the Duke appointed John Theophilus Desaguliers, the Rector of Little Stanmore. Desaguliers was already well known for his work in philosophy and for the invention of the planetarium: nevertheless, as well as his more traditional duties, he was expected to work on the mechanics of the water gardens and, according to local legend, a corpse once lay three days in the church for want of someone with the time to bury it!

The remarkable baroque interior of St Lawrence, Whitchurch, 1930s.

Despite these illustrious beginnings, the mansion of Canons survived for little more than three decades. Burdened with debt, a later Duke of Chandos decided to sell both mansion and grounds. But, unable to find a single purchaser, he allowed it to be broken up and sold piecemeal at auction in 1747.

Many of its treasures found homes elsewhere. A statue of George I was temporarily moved to Leicester Square while that of George II continues to adorn Soho's Golden Square. In the same way, carvings done for the library by Grinling Gibbons ultimately found their way to the Victoria & Albert Museum.

At auction, the principal buyer was a London cabinet-maker called William Hallett who promptly demolished the mansion, then used

William Hallett's house on the site of Canons is now a famous school.

most of its materials to create a much smaller house on the same site. It was this house that, in 1929, was purchased, together with some 10 acres of land, by today's North London Collegiate School.

In 1934 Harrow Council bought part of the original Canons estate for use as a public open space to be known as Canons Park. Later, another part of the estate, mainly the walled kitchen garden, was also acquired for a recreation ground, opened in July 1937, as the King George V Memorial Garden.

Today, as we have said, the age-old name of Canons has been perpetuated through the agency of both the Canons Park estate, whose many roads include a Canons Drive, and the Metropolitan Railway which, at the very last minute, changed the name of the station they were building from the proposed Edgware (Whitchurch Lane) to the current Canons Park.

Though his house has been gone for two and a half centuries, the Duke of Chandos himself can still be seen in effigy in the superb Chandos Mausoleum at St Lawrence, Whitchurch. Here he stands, full size, at the top of a flight of stairs – somewhat oddly attired in a Roman-style toga plus elaborate full-bottomed wig – while the figures of two of his three wives kneel in humble supplication at his feet.

It is impressive, faintly absurd and totally over-the-top – a not unfair description of Canons itself.

Daniel Dancer

Notorious
eighteenth-century
miser Daniel Dancer
counts his money.

Of all the eccentrics our town has known, the one who is best remembered – perhaps because his life is the best recorded – is the eighteenth-century Harrow Weald miser Daniel Dancer. Often described as the meanest man who ever lived, Dancer has been a constant source of interest to writers and historians; indeed, it has even been suggested that he was the model for Scrooge in Charles Dickens's *A Christmas Carol*. A history of his life appeared in print as early as 1813 while locally the *Harrow Observer* unfolded his story as a serial some ninety-seven years ago.

The fascination evidently continues, as witness Dancer's inclusion in a book entitled *English Eccentrics*, written in 1991 by the Harrow-born former BBC correspondent John Timpson.

Daniel Dancer, however, was not always the odd-ball character history records. Born in 1716, the eldest of four children of a prosperous Harrow Weald farmer, he was at one time both a conventional farmer and a respected Overseer of the Poor. Yet, following his inheritance of property that included Waldo's Farm at Uxbridge Road, Hatch End, Dancer's behaviour became increasingly bizarre.

Drawn from life by a neighbour's child, Mary Ann Bodimeade, this is considered the only true likeness of Dancer to have survived.

Soon, his 80 or so acres of land was left fallow to save the expense of cultivation while the one and only horse on the farm was allowed shoes for its hind hooves only. As for the house, Astmiss in Weald Lane, it became so tumbledown that a contemporary account said it 'had suffered so much by repair, and still wanted so much, that the most diligent antiquary could scarcely distinguish a bit of the original building'.

What makes the story even more amazing is that Dancer lacked neither family nor, it would appear, friends. For all the evident squalor of the house and the apparent unpleasantness of his person – he regarded soap as an unnecessary luxury – his sister shared his life for several decades. Inevitably, she was obliged to share his frugal lifestyle, cooking one piece of beef and fourteen dumplings every Sunday, which lasted them for the rest of the week.

Once, it is said, they discovered a dead sheep and, heedless of the cause of its death, happily augmented their diet with a quantity of home-made mutton pies. Nor did either of them allow themselves the satisfaction of a bed, choosing to sleep on straw which Dancer also used to wrap around his legs to keep out the winter cold.

Nevertheless Dancer never totally severed his links with the community and whenever there was some infringement upon Harrow Weald Common, the villagers always looked to him to lead the defence of their interests. A neighbour, Lady Tempest, seems to have taken a charitable interest in this strange brother and sister and, on one occasion, sent them a dish of trout. The problem was how it should be heated in a house where fires were never lit.

According to an oft-told story, Dancer's solution was simply to cover the dish, then sit on it until such time as he considered it was warm enough to eat!

When Miss Dancer fell ill, her brother's attitude was wholly typical. Refusing to send for a doctor, he reputedly said: 'If the old girl's time has come, the nostrums of all the quacks in Christendom cannot save her.' In the event, Miss Dancer died before she could make a will in which she evidently intended her share of the property to go to Lady Tempest in gratitude for her kindness. Instead, upon her death, her two other brothers sued for her share of the estate – whereupon Dancer himself counter-sued, claiming £30 per annum for thirty years for her board and keep. In addition, he sought an extra £100 for her last two years since 'during that time she has done nothing but eat and lie in bed'.

Though it seems hard to credit, he won his case and was granted over £1,000 for maintaining her during her lifetime.

Dancer's Harrow, as shown in a print dated 1776, was largely agricultural.

Not surprisingly, there were several attempts to rob his home. Dancer's only response was to board up the ground floor of the farm, even though this obliged him to enter and leave by an upper window using a ladder which he pulled up after him.

By now, his 'hidden' wealth was a matter of much local speculation but it was only on his death, in 1794 at the age of 78, that his home began to yield up its very real treasures. A cracked teacup was found with a note reading 'Not to be hastily overlooked' and this alone contained £600. A further £200 was discovered in the chimney. Finally, some £2,500 (then a very considerable sum) was uncovered from a dung heap while plate, table-linen, some 24 pairs of good sheets and garments of every description were all found locked away in chests.

Even in death, Dancer had one more surprise up his sleeve – it was found that he had willed his estate to Lady Tempest. But, sadly, she never lived to enjoy it, dying herself within three months of Dancer's passing.

Her sudden demise provoked yet another rumour, that she had contracted some fatal infection solely through her deathbed attendance on this most miserable, if memorable, of misers.

Edward VII

Souvenir of a royal visit to Harrow School, as printed in the *Illustrated London News* of 14 July 1894.

Though there is little comfort to be drawn from the fact, there is nothing particularly new in the twenty-first-century spectacle of a Prince of Wales who provokes rather more comment through matters of the heart than through matters of the realm.

Well over a century ago, much the same situation arose with Edward, Prince of Wales, the long-time-in-waiting heir to Queen Victoria: indeed, today he is probably remembered best for his many and colourful amorous liaisons. One such affair brought him on several occasions to Stanmore – to Warren House in Wood Lane, then the epitome of Edwardian luxury, now transformed into an Islamic Centre. The year was 1907 and the lady in question was Alice Keppel, wife to the remarkably understanding Colonel George Keppel.

By an amazing coincidence, Edward had first met Alice in 1898 at a dinner party where a fellow guest was Agnes Keyser, who had been brought up at Warren House and who, as frequently reported by the local press, had played an active part in the Stanmore social scene. Daughter of the chairman of the Colne Valley Water Company, Agnes must have made almost as strong an impression on the admittedly impressionable Edward as Alice Keppel for, shortly afterwards, she received a call from the prince's household asking if she would be willing to receive Edward and Alice for tea at her London home. Thus

The royal car arrives at Warren House, Stanmore, in June 1907.

began a series of increasingly frequent meetings at which the ever-discreet Agnes was used as cover for the royal liaison.

Our story now flashes forward some nine years, by which time Warren House had become the home of Henry Louis Bischoffsheim, an international financier married to the daughter of the Viennese court jeweller. Though Bischoffsheim was in failing health, the couple entertained lavishly and, on a June day in 1907, the prince, by now King Edward VII, was due to attend a party there, doubtless encouraged by the fact that Alice Keppel was also on the guest list.

Unlike his visit to Harrow School two years earlier (of which more anon), this was a purely private occasion and the king travelled by car with just one equerry in attendance. Unhappily, the vehicle broke down not once but twice and, though expected for lunch, the royal visitor actually arrived in the afternoon, when only a handful of spectators awaited him. Nevertheless, as the local paper reported, 'cameras were aplenty but shots were extremely difficult. It was only when the Royal party arrived at The Warren that the best pictures were obtained and, then, the motor figured most prominently' (a fact amply confirmed by the photograph opposite).

Edward, with Queen Alexandra, officially opens Harrow School's new football fields in June 1905.

Despite the unhappy journey, the king was said to be in high good humour and subsequently toured the grounds, planting a silver birch as a memento of the occasion. What's more, he stayed for what was evidently a very long dinner because, as the *Observer* reported, 'the car swung through Stanmore on its return journey as the parish clock pointed the hour of midnight'.

It is a matter of history that Alice Keppel remained Edward's special friend until his death. So, too, in a totally different way, did Agnes Keyser, and Edward was actually dining with her on the night in 1901 when he was obliged to rush to the bedside of the dying Queen Victoria. Agnes also appears to have been the very last person to entertain her monarch, since they dined together in London on 2 May 1910, just four days before his death.

In the years between, Agnes had turned her London residence into a military nursing home, running it with great efficiency under her newly chosen name of Sister Agnes. Edward apparently tried to honour this good work (as did his son, George V) but, on both occasions, Agnes Keyser politely declined. Today, however, she has a lasting memorial, for the hospital she created is still highly regarded – under the wholly appropriate name of the King Edward VII Hospital for Officers.

Edward VII also paid several official visits to Harrow School – first, with his father, the Prince Consort, and again as Prince of Wales, for the school's tercentenary celebrations in 1871. This later visit is imaginatively commemorated in one of St Mary's nine clerestory windows which provide – and it is a fact not widely known – a partial pictorial history of both church and school.

His best remembered visit, however, was for Speech Day 1905, when the school was celebrating its acquisition of 254 acres of the old Northwick estate, purchased not only to provide playing fields but also to hold back the suburban development which, even then, was threatening to engulf the Hill. The cost was some £81,579, met partly from subscription and partly from a hefty loan whose annual interest payments were personally met by Joseph Wood, an otherwise largely forgotten headmaster.

British summer weather being no respector of distinguished assemblies – the guests also included the American ambassador, the Archbishop of Canterbury and the Maharajah Gaekwar of Baroda – it rained for most of the day, slackening off just long enough for the king to move on to the terrace behind the School Chapel 'where a wireless telegraph apparatus' had been erected. By pressing a button, he was enabled to raise a flag on the far edge of the newly acquired fields.

Flambard

Dating from 1370, this memorial brass of Sir Edmund Flambard is the oldest surviving brass at St Mary's.

Which is the oldest – and most influential – name in Harrow's past? The answer might very well be Flambard, despite the fact that today the name survives only as Flambard Road in central Harrow and as a private house in Harrow Hill's High Street. For evidence of its antiquity, we need look no further than St Mary's Church on the Hill, whose earliest surviving brass (*c.* 1370) commemorates a Sir Edmund Flambard, who had charge of the army raised by the City of London for Edward III's wars against the Scots.

Earlier still, one Ranulf Flambard – almost certainly of the same family – was among the unscrupulous companions of William II who persuaded this young and weak-willed king to divert vast sums from the Church to the Crown and, in so doing, possibly delayed the building of St Mary's itself (although that's really another story for another day).

By the mid-sixteenth century, we know for sure that Flambards was the name of the Hill's grandest residence where, in about 1580, William Gerard sought to improve its facilities by connecting it to the existing well at the top of West Street. Possibly some kind of deal was struck for, at the same time that a Rectory Manor Roll licensed his domestic improvements, Gerard was permitted to enlarge the well and to erect a pump-house 'for the use of all the tenants of the Manor to draw and fetch water'.

The house now called Flambards is seen to the far right of this lithograph of the High Street from about 1830.

By the time of the English Civil Wars, Flambards was in the possession of another Gerard – Sir Gilbert of that name who, being married to a cousin of Oliver Cromwell, was widely known as a staunch Parliamentarian and a sworn opponent of Charles I. This well-established fact rather gives the lie to the age-old story whereby King Charles, fleeing for his life, stops on Harrow Hill to water his horses and to take one last look at his capital city. In fact, the tale loses even more credibility when it is recalled that, among the king's entourage at that time, were two local men, Francis Rewse of Headstone and Richard Page of Uxendon, whose allegiance to the crown had already forced them to flee the county. Nevertheless, the romantic story claimed such a hold on the Harrow imagination that, in 1925, a plaque commemorating the alleged incident was erected outside Harrow School's Art Schools at the top of Grove Hill.

Today, if you stop to read its wording, it is sensible to recall that the only truly authenticated fact is that the plaque stands at the site of one of the Hill's earliest wells, popularly known for centuries as King Charles's Well. Sadly, everything else owes more to legend than to history.

Subsequent landmarks in Flambards' history are more fully authenticated. In 1665, with twenty-five hearths, it went on record as

The Park, built on the old Flambards estate, is now one of the most handsome of Harrow School's boarding houses. *(Peter Hunter)*

the largest house in the district while, some 110 years later, it was one of the very few Hill properties to be clearly shown (as Flamberts House) in John Rocque's pioneering atlas of what we would now call suburban London.

At that time, the house stood on ground currently occupied by 27–41 London Road. It was from this site that, in 1768, the then owner Francis Herne began a series of improvements to both house and grounds that brought to Harrow the most famous of landscape gardeners, 'Capability' Brown. (He had actually been christened Lancelot but his propensity to see 'capabilities' in virtually every project he was offered earned him the nickname by which he is still best known).

From surviving bills, we know that Brown worked on the project between 1768 and 1771 and charged Herne some £12,000, a huge sum for the day. But his work included the creation of a lake of considerable dimensions and, having completed commissions at Blenheim Palace and Chatsworth, he was at the very height of his fame.

In the late 1790s, Richard Page, already a noted Wembley landowner, inherited Flambards under the will of his sister, Mrs Mary Herne, and began building himself a new mansion, substantially the building we know today as the Harrow School boarding house, The Park. It was still unfinished in 1803 when the estate was purchased by the 2nd Baron Northwick who had the means to decorate its walls with Old Masters; indeed, works by, among others, Raphael, Titian, Caravaggio and Watteau can still be seen in an 1823 auction catalogue held at Harrow Civic Centre Library.

As for the original Flambards, much of its site was later taken up by the Edward Prior-designed mansion Manor Lodge, pulled down in the 1950s and replaced by a row of maisonettes. At this remove it is hard to say whether even a trace of the original Flambards has survived, although expert eyes claim to detect Tudor brickwork in the ruined folly which can still be seen at the end of Harrow Park, a private road which undoubtedly formed part of the original Flambards estate. Certainly, the Coadestone lion (part of the Northwick coat of arms), which once guarded the garden frontage, remains for all to see, since it is now embedded above a window on The Park's High Street façade.

Nor has the name Flambards been completely lost to the Hill, currently being used for a charming Grade II listed house at 11 High Street. By comparison with its illustrious forebears, however, this Flambards is something of a Johnny-come-lately, dating only from the late eighteenth century!

Grim's Dyke

The south-west front of Grim's Dyke, home to two famous artists.

Royal Academician Frederick Goodall in about 1863. The mansion was first built on his instructions.

Grim's Dyke and Sir William Gilbert are so inextricably linked these days that it comes as something of a surprise to realise that this most famous of Harrow Weald mansions was not actually built for the celebrated partner of Sir Arthur Sullivan but for another and very different Victorian artist. This was the painter Frederick Goodall – the son of Turner's engraver – who, as early as 1856 (a full thirty-four years before Gilbert's arrival), acquired the 100-acre estate from the Marquess of Abercorn; he was, however, unable to build immediately because Charles Blackwell, the local landowner and member of the Crosse & Blackwell grocery firm, still had a lease on the land.

As it happened, the delay allowed Goodall to amass even more wealth from his immensely fashionable paintings, largely of colourful Middle Eastern scenes. By 1869, Goodall was thus able to commission Richard Norman Shaw to build a truly impressive house on the Harrow Weald land which had earlier taken its name from the possibly Iron Age earthworks cutting across it. Shaw (a pupil of Charles Cockerell, who had redesigned Old Schools for Harrow School in the 1820s) was then making something of a reputation as a designer of highly ornamental homes for the so-called 'artist-princes' of the day and, according to Goodall, gave much thought to his design to make it 'as picturesque as possible'.

Goodall himself added much to the picturesqueness of its exterior, not least by importing whole herds of Egyptian sheeps and goats which served the double purpose of amusing his guests and acting as a model for later Egyptian-style landscapes. By 1882, however, Goodall was telling his friends that it was 'a disadvantage for an artist to live entirely in the country' and Grim's Dyke was sold to Robert Heriot, a partner in Hambro's Bank. The banker lived there for the next eight years so it was not until 1891, after many alterations had been made, that the house's most famous occupant moved in. Sir William Gilbert was, by then, immensely famous and wealthy from his partnership with Sullivan which had already produced an unrivalled series of still-performed comic operas such as *The Mikado*, *The Gondoliers* and *The Pirates of Penzance*.

Adopting the lavish lifestyle of a country squire, he soon acquired a staff of at least twenty indoor and outdoor servants. Gilbert's irrepressible if somewhat schoolboyish jesting was widely demonstrated at Grim's Dyke where his horses were called Bryant and May after the match company (they were, you see, a perfect match) and he christened his loudly braying donkey Adelina Patti, after the contemporary opera star. Only in court, where he served as a local magistrate for many years, did he have to curb his humour.

A big man (6ft 4in), Gilbert liked to excel in all manly pursuits and was both an able tennis player and an enthusiatic early motorist, keeping in his stables a fine collection of cars including both a Rolls-Royce and a Cadillac. Sadly, another enthusiasm – for swimming in the lake in his grounds – brought about his untimely death. Towards the end of May 1911, the 74-year-old Gilbert drove to Harrow station to meet a friend, Winifred Emery, and her seventeen-year-old niece, Ruby Preece, with the idea of taking them swimming. But once she was in the water, young Ruby quickly got into difficulties. Gallantly, Gilbert went to her rescue but while she was holding on to his shoulders, as instructed, he suddenly sank from view.

Taken from the lake by his gardeners, Gilbert was found to be dead. There was no post-mortem but at an inquest, hurriedly arranged in the billiards room, the jury returned a verdict of Accidental Death, after hearing a doctor say that he had no doubt death had been caused by 'syncope of the heart' (basically, a fainting fit) brought on by over-exertion.

After a lavish funeral, to which over 300 wreaths were sent, Sir William Gilbert's ashes were laid to rest in a tomb at St John's, Stanmore. Lady Gilbert lived on at Grim's Dyke with Nancy, their adopted daughter, until her own death in 1936, but the lake was closed off and partially drained.

As for Ruby (later known as Patricia) Preece, she was to achieve further notoriety when the artist Stanley Spencer divorced his first wife to marry her. In the event, they never lived together, Preece choosing to remain in an existing lesbian relationship.

W.S. Gilbert in his Grim's Dyke library, drawn for the *Daily Mirror* in 1904.

For a while, at least, Grim's Dyke shared the fate of many big and unwieldy properties, becoming a medical rehabilitation centre. By then, too, it had acquired 'the old dark house' appearance beloved of film-makers and was occasionally used as a setting for horror films starring

Hotel staff lay the tables for tea on the terrace, July 2004.

such luminaries as Boris Karloff and Vincent Price. Then, in 1969, its current owners, the Greater London Council, granted Harrow Council a 999-year lease with the stipulation that, were the house to be converted for hotel use, the Gilbertian links must be retained.

As a great many readers will know, this promise is now being handsomely honoured at the popular Grim's Dyke Hotel.

Hospitals

Diana Churchill (left), daughter of Old Harrovian Sir Winston, opens Harrow Hospital's Nursing Home in October 1930.

Given that the letter 'H' is now the recognised symbol for a hospital, it seems highly appropriate that the eighth entry in our alphabet should concern the borough's healthcare.

For a start, it's worth reminding ourselves that Harrow – especially the Hill – has long been regarded as a healthier place than its lower-lying neighbours. Certainly, many reports over the centuries confirm its use as a place of refuge from the plagues and other ills that once beset London; for example, in 1537, Richard Layton, then Rector of Harrow, was able to promise his mentor, Thomas Cromwell, twenty beds in the town 'where there has been no sickness in a year'.

Judging from published memoirs, the families of many Harrow School boys were also attracted by the thought of their boys being educated at 'high and healthy Harrow'. Among them were the parents of Winston Churchill who, despite the fact that boys from the Marlborough family usually went to Thameside Eton, chose the drier atmosphere of the Hill for their son who was then far from the robust figure of later years.

In one way, at least, the tradition persists even to this day for the robed figure on the Borough's official coat-of-arms is that of Hygeia, the Goddess of Health.

Yet even the healthiest town must have its occasional accident and illness and, in default of any earlier records, we know that in 1773 two public-spirited parishioners of St Mary's, Harrow on the Hill, caused a small infirmary to be built on Sudbury Common. Three-quarters of a century later, this pest-house, as it was known, had become so dilapidated that demolition seemed the only solution, adding weight to public pressure for a new and 'modern' hospital.

This duly opened in February 1866, although the building, in truth, was merely a conversion of two cottages at the bottom of Roxeth Hill. As such, it was able to offer only nine beds with just one full-time nurse in attendance. The rest of the work was carried out by a voluntary team led by Constance Hewlett, daughter of Thomas Hewlett, the town doctor, who himself had done much to improve the Hill's drainage and sanitation some seventeen years before. The cottages, however, had been secured only on a short-term lease and two years later the landlady gave the hospital workers notice to quit.

Happily, a benefactor called Charles Leaf came to the rescue, offering a piece of land in Lower Road if enough money could be raised to put a hospital on it. Enthusiastic fund-raising continued until 1872 by which time there was sufficient money for the erection of Harrow's first (supposedly) custom-built hospital.

As our picture shows, it looked more like a pleasant family home than a hospital and, although welcomed at the time, there is little doubt that

its general layout was wholly unsuited to its purpose. Years later its secretary, Dr A.H.Williams, told the local paper that 'it was hard to believe it had been designed as a hospital . . . The wards, small and inconvenient, were on three floors and the staircase, steep, narrow and winding, had newels projecting above the banisters so that it was impossible to carry patients to the upper rooms with safety and comfort.'

Dr Williams was equally critical of the fact that patients due for operations had first to be carried through the female ward and that the solitary male WC was 'situated in a cupboard under the staircase in the middle of the hall'.

Certainly by today's standards the hospital's regime was unbelievably tough on the patients. A copy of the In-Patient Regulations for the year 1896, which I recently found at the Civic Centre Library, makes it abundantly plain that patients (or presumably their relatives) 'will be responsible for the washing of their own clothes'. They were also expected to assist in housework, needlework and gardening!

In those pre-NHS days, of course, the sick had to pay for their hospital care although the charges (roughly scaled according to income) could hardly be considered excessive. In-patients 'belonging to the labouring class' paid 9*d* a week while 'the class of small shop-keepers and mechanics' paid 1*s*. Interestingly enough, domestic servants – of which there would have been a great many running the Hill's bigger houses – were charged double the shop-keeper rate, presumably on the understanding that most, if not all, of the money would be paid by their employers.

Any patients who felt like complaining obviously had to curb their tongues, for the Regulations state that 'profane, abusive and immoral language will be punished by dismissal from the house' (though it is difficult to know how this could ever have worked in practice). Even the patients' reading matter was vetted, for a further rule lays down that 'the nurse will allow no book or publication in the wards, except such as are sanctioned by the Vicar of Harrow'.

Having opened at a time of considerable growth for the town, this hospital's limited facilities were quickly overstretched, not least in the treatment of infectious diseases. In the event, the inadvertent admission of a smallpox case meant that an entire ward had to be closed down, repainted and whitewashed, and its bedding and furniture renewed.

The obvious solution was to build a separate isolation hospital and, in 1894, a small specialist unit arose in the Roxbourne area primarily 'for the reception of cases of scarlet fever, diphtheria, enteric fever and

The later and much-loved hospital on Roxeth Hill, *c.* 1907.

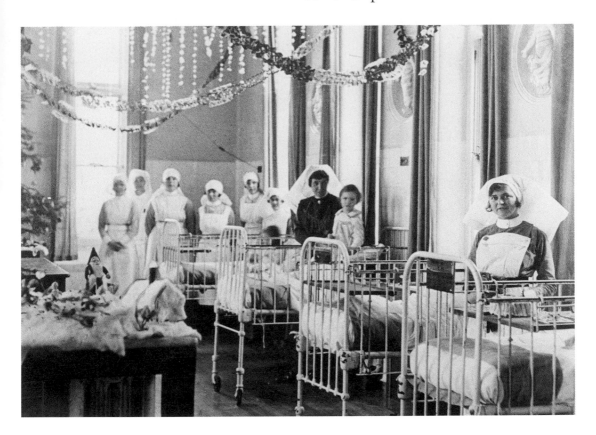

Asiatic cholera'. Surviving reports suggest that its discipline was even more rigid than that of the Lower Road hospital, although patients might have derived some comfort from the dietary list, which as published in 1895 allowed those on the so-called full diet to have four ounces of suet pudding three times a week!

Towards the beginning of the twentieth century, plans were laid for the construction of a much bigger hospital, which subsequently became the much-admired Arnold Mitchell-designed Harrow Hospital at the top of Roxeth Hill. Dr Williams' two sons, Sam and John, had the privilege of cutting the first sod on the site, an event recorded in a photograph in my possession but one which, sadly, has faded too much to permit its reproduction in these pages.

As the town continued to grow, so, too, did this new Cottage Hospital, for its site had sensibly been chosen to permit future expansion. In 1925, a children's ward was opened, followed in 1931 by a major extension known as the Stuart Memorial Wing (after a dedicated supporter). The opening was attended by the late Queen Mother whose husband, then Duke of York, used a golden key to enter the premises for the very first time. The day's ceremonials included a special service in

Christmas 1929, in Harrow Hospital's children's ward.

Harrow Hospital staff relax in the snow, c. 1932.

Harrow School Speech Room for which – at a time of rigid social divisions – it is interesting to read that 'invitations have been issued with a large-hearted regard to all who love to work for the hospital'.

The previous year, Diana Churchill, daughter of Sir Winston, opened a nurses' home on Roxeth Hill, an acquisition followed later in the decade by the purchase (again for staff accommodation) of the large old vicarage that once belonged to Christ Church, Roxeth.

The more recent history of this much loved institution must, inevitably, be telescoped given the space available. Suffice it to say that, by the time of the opening of the present Northwick Park Hospital in the Watford Road in 1970, its glory days were obviously at an end, although it continued to provide geriatric care right up to its closure in 1998.

The inevitable redevelopment of the site has been a long and painful process, already marked by two public inquiries which sought, with only minimal success, to limit the developers' ambitious (some said greedy) plans.

Even as you read these words, the original Arnold Mitchell block of 1906 is being turned into apartments while all around it rises totally new residential development – in all, some 99 properties plus a YMCA hostel earmarked for the site of the former Nurses' Home.

Industry

Knocking-off
time at Kodak,
c. 1929.

Industry is not the first thing you think of in connection with Harrow, which was, after all, a largely agricultural community for centuries. Neverthless from the 1880s on, its improved communications and its proximity to London attracted a number of soon-to-be-famous businesses, at least two of which remain to this day.

Curiously enough, it was a very different asset – the district's clear air – which first caught the attention of George Eastman, the founder of the US-based Kodak photographic company. Conscious that the level of dust must be kept to a minimum in certain sensitive production areas, Eastman chose a smallish site in unpolluted Wealdstone for his very first overseas operation.

In 1891, Kodak (whose name was created by Eastman himself because it could be readily pronounced anywhere in the world) started off with just two production buildings separated by a power house. More surprisingly, there was also a shed for about 100 chickens, not to supply the works canteen (although Kodak were among the very first to introduce such staff facilities) but to produce the egg-white then

An aerial view of the Kodak factory, probably in the 1950s.

needed for making the albumen paper exclusively used for contact printing. Later, the original site was extended to some 55 acres on which there were ultimately over 100 separate buildings, making Kodak the largest private employer in the district for many decades.

One reason for their success was that, from the earliest days, a great variety of jobs was open to women and, since the factory itself was a clean and inviting place in which to work, many girls preferred to walk miles across the fields to Kodak rather than continue in less congenial employment elsewhere. The uncomfortably hot local laundries (see p. 48) were among the greatest losers.

The sheer scale of the Kodak operation – it even had its own fire brigade at one period – presented considerable problems on the outbreak of the Second World War, not least the necessity to fix black-out material to every single window. In the event, the premises never received a direct hit although on one occasion what appeared to be a parachute was found draped – appropriately enough – over the tail fin of a captured German Messerschmitt displayed for propaganda reasons on the sports field just across the road. The parachute was quickly found to be attached to a land mine which, fortunately, had failed to explode on landing.

Just one year after Kodak's arrival in Headstone Drive, a Belfast-based publishing company, David Allen and Sons, opened a massive printing works in the same street. Later, they added a 100ft power-house chimney, with their name in giant letters running from top to bottom. In July 1906, a *Harrow Observer* reporter was hauled by pulley to the very top from which viewpoint it seemed that 'Wealdstone had become microscopic, toy trains ran beneath on railway lines and groups of dwarfs ran fussily about the ground'.

David Allen quickly won an enviable reputation, especially in the production of theatrical posters. When the First World War broke out, they were proficient enough to be taken over for the production of the nation's ration books. Later still, they were requisitioned by the government for the use of the Stationery Office and, from 1920 onwards, the Wealdstone premises officially assumed

Inside David Allen's printing works, 1896.

the title of His Majesty's Stationery Office. The original David Allen company moved to Wandsworth, while HMSO continued in Wealdstone until the building's closure in the 1980s. Harrow's Crown Court was ultimately built on much the same site.

In the last decade of the nineteenth century, Wealdstone also welcomed Winsor & Newton, formed some 65 years earlier by chemists and painters, William Winsor and Henry Newton, inventors of the first watercolour paints that could be lifted directly by the application of a wet brush. When Winsor later invented the screw-cap paint tube, their success was guaranteed: indeed, some 100 or so years after their arrival, the company still has a thriving business locally, trading under the name of Colart Fine Art & Graphics.

Having acquired a top name in paint, in 1898 Wealdstone attracted the Hamilton Brush Company, which was soon calling itself, with some justification, 'the world's leading brush manufacturers' and which remained a prominent local employer right through to 1990.

Not all the early arrivals, however, were so successful. Having almost certainly moved to Wealdstone to be near the railway, gunsmiths Cogswell & Harrison, had the misfortune for a spark from a passing train to fall through their roof and ignite a quantity of woodshavings. The company never truly recovered from the resultant fire and subsequently moved elsewhere.

In rather more propitious circumstances, fire came back to Wealdstone in 1923 when the much-admired Whitefriars Glass Company decided to move from the City of London to the suburbs. As their name suggests, the company originated on the site of an old monastery belonging to the white-robed Carmelites on which a furnace had been burning unquenched since 1680. Rather than break with tradition, a lighted brazier from the old works was then carried through the streets to the Wealdstone premises in order to ignite the new furnace.

Specialising in ecclesiastical stained glass, for which noted artists such as Dante Gabriel Rossetti and Edward Burne-Jones created designs, Whitefriars continued to prosper until a late twentieth-century decline in church commissions brought about their closure in 1982.

Ethel Jayne

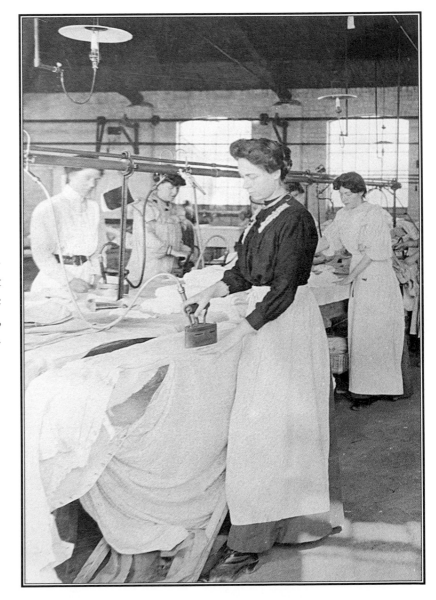

Early twentieth-century ironers at work at Little Laundries, Wealdstone.

Among the agreeable aspects of writing about some of the less familiar aspects of Harrow's past is the opportunity it gives to pay belated tribute to long-forgotten personalities who, in their day, were genuine pioneers. One such was Miss Ethel Jayne who, during the early years of the twentieth century, did much to advance the techniques utilised in that least glamorous, but most essential, of businesses: the laundry.

Even in these air-conditioned days, summer working in office or shop can often seem unbearably stuffy. So one can only imagine what a summer's day must have been like in an old-style hand laundry, where the dirty linen was boiled in vast coppers and the ironing done manually with heavy flat-irons, especially as the employees were expected to wear the sort of clothing shown in our illustrations. Nevertheless Miss Jayne's management skills were such that she invariably managed to hold a good team together at the Little Laundries which she ran from premises in Stuart Road, Wealdstone.

Word of her success obviously spread to high places for, when the First World War broke out in 1914 – and, for the first time, women

Miss E.B. Jayne drives her pony and trap to the laundry she established in 1907.

were mobilised for war-work – David Lloyd George, then Minister of Munitions, found her a very special job. This was no less than the recruitment and control of the thousands of women required to maintain Britain's munitions factories.

Although at one time Miss Jayne had as many as 200,000 women in her charge, she performed beyond all expectations and, once the Armistice had been declared, a grateful nation awarded her an OBE, one of the very first ever to be given to a woman.

Back in the Wealdstone laundry, she was quick to realise that North America had now taken Britain's earlier lead in laundering techniques. Soon she was touring the United States and Canada, enabling her to bring her business right up to date through the introduction of the very latest devices. The float-roll ironer, in particular, proved a triumph, offering for the first time a machine finish virtually as good as that previously obtained only by expensive, time-consuming handwork.

Throughout her reign Miss Jayne's interest in the business extended to every single detail, even the horse-drawn delivery vehicles, for which she introduced a prize for the best turned-out horse and van.

It seems entirely possible that she was also responsible for her company's advertising, which was based around the highly apt slogan 'Little and Good'. A surviving advertisement, to be seen in Harrow's Local History Collection, vividly conjures up the leisured lifestyle then enjoyed by many Harrow ladies. There, high in a list of 'Reasons Why You Should Send Your Linen To Us', Miss Jayne declares: 'Because we are careful with the maids' clothes.'

Away from the laundry, the great passion of Miss Jayne's life centred around ponies. Apart from the pony and trap in which she normally drove herself to work from her home in Stanmore, she maintained a whole string of ponies which were regularly entered for – and occasionally won – the then-famous Northolt Pony Derby.

Under her very personal control, Miss Jayne's business continued to prosper until, inevitably, it was taken over by a much larger concern. This was the mammoth Advance Laundries which, as late as the 1970s, had major contracts with most of the big London hotels. By then, of course, Miss Jayne had long since died, having been carried off by a chill picked up during an early springtime visit in 1940 to . . . where else but the Northolt Park Race Course?

In contrast to Miss Jayne's record of success, it seems worth noting that some other local laundries of the late nineteenth and early twentieth centuries staggered from one misfortune to another. The Harrow School Laundry in Alma Road, South Harrow, in particular, had great difficulty in finding suitable workers.

Inside the Stuart
Road packing
department.

Harrow's Local History Collection houses the school laundry's annual report for 1881 in which the Laundry Committee's chairman unfolds a whole catalogue of catastrophes, beginning with a serious injury to the Foreman of the Wash House 'whose life was, for some time, in danger'. The report continues: 'The Foreman who succeeded him brought the highest testimonials and was thought to prove a treasure.' Instead, he was quickly sacked for incompetence 'but not before his bad washing had so injured the colour of much of the linen that it took weeks to bring it back to even a moderately good condition'.

Ruefully, the chairman continues: 'It has been found necessary to change all the heads of department, the Manageress once, the Engineer three times, the Foreman of the Wash House three times and the Forewoman of Ironers three times.' Nevertheless he still considered the school was right to have its own laundry since it ensured control over 'otherwise irresponsible and reckless washerwomen'.

In any event, one feels that all their problems could have been quickly resolved had they been able to discover another Ethel Jayne!

The King's Head

The King's Head in 1905. By this time the hotel had acquired neighbouring shops, including a hairdresser.

How sad to think that, very soon, only the seniors among Harrow residents will know the exact spot where the King's Head hotel served the community for at least four centuries. For, even as this volume goes to print, the once-famous hostelry is being transformed into a residential complex, far, far bigger than the original hotel. It even has a new name, Kings Gate, though no-one seems to have pointed out to the developers that there already exists a splendid pair of houses at the top of Sudbury Hill which, for over a century, have been called Queensgate and Kingsgate!

Ironically, for a building at the very top of Harrow Hill, the King's Head could be said to have been going downhill for years; ever since a feckless landlord permitted the kind of customers and conduct that ultimately lost him his licence and, later, his liberty!

In more recent times, the hotel has served as a kind of refugee hostel, a usage which, while it created no nuisance for local residents, did nothing to prevent the property's deterioration. In the circumstances, development was probably inevitable; nevertheless, as many residents told a public enquiry, they would have preferred a new hotel to the presence of apartments and houses on so historic a site.

In Edwardian times, the former coaching inn was a popular starting point for horse-drawn outings.

Just how historic remains a matter of conjecture. For centuries, the old building carried on its façade the date 1535 which seems to date its foundation to the middle of the reign of King Henry VIII. And, of course, it is Henry's portrait that has always appeared on the inn sign. Yet the first printed reference historians have been able to find to the Harrow hotel is in a St Mary's Vestry Minute Book of August 1706. Nor does any licensee appear to be listed before 1719.

The so-called King's Head Green was little more than a scruffy patch of grass in 1905, as seen here.

The one totally secure link between Harrow and Henry is that, in 1545, Archbishop Cranmer, then Lord of the Archbishop's Manor of Harrow, was obliged to surrender the manor to his king. But, in the event, Henry only retained it for a matter of months before granting it to a royal favourite, Sir Edward North, an action which hardly suggests any especial interest or affection for the place.

Yet, over the years, more and more Tudor legends have accrued to the building. Only a year or so ago, I found myself on Radio 4's *You and Yours* arguing against a Pinner resident totally convinced that the hotel was originally a royal hunting lodge; moreover, one that had a secret escape tunnel running from its cellar, allegedly built to enable the lusty monarch to make a quick exit, possibly during his courtship of Mistress Anne Boleyn.

At the end of the nineteenth century appliances at Harrow's newly built fire station were drawn by horses from the King's Head Stables (far right).

Not only have no records of a royal lodge survived, the Boleyn connection can be easily disposed of, particularly if 1535 is accepted as the year of the inn's foundation as, by that date, the provocative Anne was already Henry's queen. (A year later, of course, a disenchanted husband sent her to the block.)

As for the tunnel, there is certainly some kind of underground passageway beneath the building and extending under the present adjoining shops, but its origins could be as mundane as an extended cellar space: certainly, when a reporter from the *Harrow Observer* was shown the King's Head in 1971, he described the cellars as 'dark and dank and of little interest'.

From my own (modest) researches, it seems that the hotel has generally tended to soft-pedal the Henry VIII connections. Even when the place was put up for auction in 1900, the advertisements variously referred to 'that celebrated historical property' and 'its historic associations' without saying just what those associations were.

What is unarguable is the unique position the King's Head occupied in local life, especially during the early nineteenth century, when the town of Harrow meant Harrow on the Hill. (Greenhill, today's Central Harrow, was then just a small hamlet on the lower ground.)

It was at the King's Head in 1849 that the townsfolk – doubtless holding handkerchiefs to their noses – gave evidence to the General Board of Health's inspector, which paved the way for the town's first proper drainage and sanitation system. It was here, too, just a few years later, that the local great and good celebrated the arrival of gaslight, partying in a ballroom brilliantly lit, as the press described it, 'by the new illuminant'. Nor would the fire station of 1880 ever have been built without the assurance that the neighbouring King's Head stables would provide sufficient horses to pull the brigade's machines.

The inn's importance at this time is further emphasised by the frequency with which it features in the reminiscences of distinguished Old Boys of Harrow School (for all that licensed premises were supposedly strictly out of bounds to the boys). For example, in his autobiographical *Annals of my Life*, Charles Wordsworth, a nineteenth-century Bishop of St Alban's, recalls how he and his school friend Manning – later the famous Cardinal Manning – were being entertained to champagne by two midshipmen in the King's Head gardens when Dr George Butler, their headmaster, arrived with his wife. 'So up sprang Manning and I like startled harts,' Wordsworth writes, and, quick as lightning, 'rushed over the hedge which was close at hand, dashed down the back side of the garden and escaped into Hog Lane [now West Street] undetected.'

In 1974 the King's Head still had a much appreciated garden extending far down the Hill.

During the summer of 2004 the hotel became one vast plastic-wrapped building site.

The inn is also the source of many entertaining anecdotes in an 1880s book by the Revd H. Torre. For all its cumbersome title, *Recollections of School Days At Harrow More Than 50 Years Ago*, this is a particularly lively and honest account of the sometimes cruel mischief perpetrated by the boys. Chief among their victims were the Cockney visitors to the Hill who, in summertime, regularly arrived at the King's Head with hired horses and traps ready to enjoy a day in what was then rightly considered 'the country'.

On arrival, the King's Head grooms would sensibly mark each trap with a number and then chalk the same number on its horses' hooves. But, once the grooms were out of sight, the boys would turn up with fresh chalk, rub out the original numbers and replace them with new numbers of their own invention. Writes Torre gleefully, if somewhat unfeelingly: 'As these vehicles and horses were mostly hired for the Sunday, and were quite unknown to their respective drivers, the confusion on their return to their homes in London may easily be imagined.'

The stables, of course, have long since vanished and, by the time you read this, the hotel will have gone the same way. Only a partially preserved façade will remain to remind us that this was, for centuries, one of the best-known and best-loved buildings in our borough.

Lowlands

Lowlands' most celebrated occupant, Isabella Rotch, pictured in 1901 at the age of 92.

When anyone refers to Lowlands today, they are almost invariably talking about the busy Lowlands Road (at the rear of Harrow Metropolitan station) or the adjoining Lowlands Recreation Ground. In fact, they both take their name from – and, indeed, both originally belonged to – the estate of a handsome nineteenth-century villa, whose attractions even earned a mention in that impressive publication *The Beauties of Middlesex.*

If you take the trouble to look, the villa still stands today, although over the last few decades it has become increasingly dwarfed by the multiple buildings that now make up Harrow College. When it was built in 1820, the house was called Cassetta Cottage and stood on the site of a much older cottage almost certainly belonging to The Grove, the great house at the top of Harrow Hill (after which the nearby Grove Open Space is named).

Lowlands was the name given to it by its most famous occupant, the remarkably gifted Benjamin Rotch, who must have found tranquil Harrow a very happy contrast to his early years spent in Paris at the time of the blood-soaked French Revolution. So great was the danger

The original Lowlands Villa as it looked in 1976 before the encroachment of other departments of what is now Harrow College.

to all but ardent revolutionaries that at one time he was apparently smuggled out of the city hidden in an empty flour barrel. Rotch was a barrister by profession, and became successively a magistrate, an MP and Deputy Lieutenant for Middlesex. He owed much of his considerable wealth to his inventions, including a highly successful lever whose design he patented.

Harrow Girls County School, which originally opened on the Lowlands estate in 1913.

To 'the pretty villa of Lowlands' in 1828 Benjamin Rotch brought his 19-year-old bride, Isabella, and it was probably for her amusement that he later staged the Harrow Carousel, a medieval-inspired equestrian entertainment, whose horseback parade of lance-carrying ladies can currently be seen in a mural at the Civic Centre.

Around the 1860s, he also established a hydropathic bath (roughly where Station Road meets College Road) to which the ailing flocked for a so-called 'water cure'. He even had a medal struck (and this can still be seen at our Headstone Manor Museum) showing a winged figure hovering encouragingly over a reclining invalid; however, whether such medals were actually given to celebrate cures or merely to mark attendance at the baths is no longer clear.

Although Rotch lived at Lowlands for a full 27 years, Isabella was to outlive him by more than half a century. In 1882, when she was already in her seventies, she had a window installed at St Mary's, Harrow on the Hill, in memory of their only son who had died in infancy, some fifty years before.

In 1908 she celebrated her centenary, delighting a local press representative with her lively recollections of such events as the return of the wounded from the battle of Waterloo, the opening of Harrow's first railway station (in 1836) and the great fire at The Grove in 1888. This, she remembered, 'because the feathers from the boys' beds floated down the Hill and made things uncomfortable at Lowlands'.

On her 100th birthday, Isabella Rotch entertained a string of distinguished visitors, among them Dr Henry Montagu Butler, Head Master of Harrow, one of seven such heads she had claimed as her friends.

In her later years, she was also frequently visited by the then Vicar of Harrow, the Revd Edgar Stogdon, who claimed that the old lady had been much concerned about a recurrent dream in which she saw her house and garden filled with scores of identically clad girls. Isabella Rotch was well on the way to her 101st birthday when she died. Amazingly enough, within four years her recurrent dream came true when Lowlands became the first Harrow Girls' County Grammar School.

Early histories of the school suggest that the first pupils were much intrigued by Lowlands. A room with a barred window so much reminded them of a cell that rumours spread that Lowlands had been an overnight stop on the road to Tyburn, the notorious gallows at Marble Arch, where many criminals were hanged. Although there is a short road called Tyburn Lane only a few yards away, the cell was probably one that had been constructed during Rotch's days as a local magistrate when the house (or more likely its lodge) occasionally served as a police court. Similarly, investigations of a mysterious tunnel thought to lead to St Mary's Church on the Hill revealed nothing more exciting than extensive cellars.

One significant change, however, was quickly made to the house. The twin stone eagles decorating the lodge, being considered more suitable for a boys' school than a girls', were promptly transported up the hill. Here they (or replicas since the originals were stolen a few years back) still stand guard over the entrance to Bradbys, the Harrow School boarding house in the High Street.

Jessie Matthews

The popular
musical star, with
John Mills, in her
1932 film
The Midshipmaid.

It seems doubly appropriate to choose the 1920s and '30s musical star Jessie Matthews as the 'unlucky thirteenth' entrant in our alphabet, for her name not only begins with the thirteenth letter but her life (much of which was lived in or around our borough) was constantly shadowed by bad luck and bad health.

One of eleven children, Jessie was born into relative poverty in Soho in 1907 and is said to have earned her first much-needed pennies by dancing in the streets. With her dancing ability, striking looks and bell-toned singing voice, she was clearly equipped for stardom except that, at a time when virtually all British stage and screen stars were expected to speak with a cut-glass accent, her speech was the purest Cockney. And so, in real life, Jessie underwent the kind of transformation which George Bernard Shaw wrote about in *Pygmalion*, itself later transformed into the musical *My Fair Lady*.

'Refained' – some would say to the point of affectation – Jessie quickly became the all-singing, all-dancing star of West End musicals for which composers as famous as the American duo of Rodgers and Hart wrote especially for her. The cinema beckoned and she was soon lighting up the British screen in films such as *The Midshipmaid* (with John Mills), *The Good Companions* (with John Gielgud) and, especially, *Evergreen*, based on her biggest stage success. Her co-star was the comedian Sonnie Hale, who was to become the second of her three husbands.

During his British studio years, Alfred Hitchcock directed her in his (admittedly little remembered) musical, *Waltzes From Vienna*. Hollywood seemed the next logical step but, although she travelled to California to star opposite the then very famous Robert Montgomery, the film was never made. Later still, a plan to co-star her with Fred Astaire also came to nothing when her theatrical producers refused to release her from a current West End contract.

There were, too, recurrent health problems and it is now widely accepted that, throughout her career, she was a fairly regular patient at a well-known psychiatric clinic on Harrow on the Hill.

Long a resident of Northwood (where she had bought her parents a home), Jessie Matthews made a triumphant appearance in Harrow in October 1937, when she opened the Granada cinema in Sheepcote Road. Those who know it today only as the converted Gold's Gym may be surprised to learn that it was once one of the jewels in the Granada circuit's crown, a 2,222-seater 'picture palace', designed by the very fashionable Theodore Komisarjevsky who, in the event, had to telephone most of his instructions from a Swiss sanatorium where he was recovering from pneumonia.

According to the local press, the presence of Jessie Matthews and Sonnie Hale and the Band of the Royal Scots Guards saw huge crowds assembled long before the doors had opened 'and police and commissionaires had to join together to control the excited film-goers'. But then, the whole gala evening, complete with a double bill of films and a recital on the Mighty Wurlitzer organ, cost only 9*d* for a seat in the stalls!

The opening film was Gracie Fields in *The Show Goes On* – a highly appropriate epithet for Jessie Matthews and her film career in the 1930s. But by the beginning of the next decade, changes in popular taste, brought about in part by the Second World War, and the star's propensity to put on weight, saw fewer film roles coming her way. An exception was the MGM musical, *Tom Thumb*, although the once glamorous Jessie now portrayed Tom's homely mother.

GRANADA STATION ROAD **HARROW**
please pronounce it GRA-NAH-DAH

Grand Opening by **JESSIE MATTHEWS & SONNIE HALE in person**

Monday Oct 25 at 7.30 p.m

DOORS OPEN AT 7   THEN DAILY FROM 12.30

the wonder theatre of 1938

A local press advertisement for the opening of Harrow's Granada ('please pronounce it GRA-NAH-DAH').

With her career in the doldrums, Jessie was effectively rescued by the BBC which, in 1963, cast her in the title role of the radio series, *Mrs Dale's Diary*. It was an instant success, and she went on to make over 1,500 appearances in a role which older listeners still recall with affection.

In her later years, Jessie Matthews moved from Northwood to Harrow, finally living with a sister at 154 Uxbridge Road. It was here that she contracted the cancer which caused her death in 1975. Further stresses in an always difficult life became apparent on the reading of her will. It ignored her adopted daughter, Catherine, leaving most of her estate in trust to Jessica, an under-age grandchild.

Michael Thornton, who wrote a well-received biography of the star, believes that it was Jessica who was ultimately responsible for placing the present memorial plaque in the Garden of Rest at the parish church of St Martin's, Ruislip.

Very simple, as our photograph shows, it gives just her name – Jessie Margaret Matthews OBE – her dates and a reference to the Old Testament Book of Ecclesiastes. Anyone bothering to check will discover that the reference is to that familiar sequence of words beginning 'To everything there is a season'. The passage continues, with a rather chilling aptness, given the turbulent nature of Jessie's

The modest semi-detached house where Jessie Matthews spent her final years.

life, 'a time to weep and a time to laugh, a time to mourn and a time to dance'.

Happily, to an older generation, it is the dancing they most remember, recalled in recent years by a spate of film retrospectives, TV programmes, books, even a recent musical of her life called, after one of her favourite songs, 'Over My Shoulder'. Premiered at The Old Mill at Sonning, it attracted notices and audiences strong enough to warrant a transfer to the much larger Greenwich Theatre and, ultimately if briefly, to the West End where the real Jessie sparkled for so long.

Already fading, this plaque in a Ruislip churchyard is the only local reminder of a favourite star.

Nelson's Illegitimate Daughter

The child Horatia – born of the naval hero's liaison with Lady Hamilton.

Most Harrovians with a taste for local history probably know that Lord Byron had an illegitimate daughter who is buried in our town. In comparison, very few seem to be aware that Lord Nelson's love-child, Horatia, not only spent her final years in Pinner but is also buried there, in Paines Lane cemetery.

This is just what Horatia herself would have wanted because, for most of her adult life, she wisely chose to ignore the illustrious parentage which had caused her so much heartache. Horatia was born of Horatio Nelson's liaison with the notorious Emma, Lady Hamilton, wife of Sir William Hamilton, one of his oldest friends. What's more, at the time of her birth, the great naval hero was still officially married. Both parents, therefore, became involved in an increasingly elaborate plan of concealment.

First, Horatia, while less than a week old, was secretly handed over to a Mrs Gibson, a Marylebone-based nurse, with no information given as to her identity except the name Horatia. (This in itself, one would have thought, was something of a giveaway, particularly as the *Oxford Dictionary of Christian Names* thinks it unlikely that a female form of Horatio had been known previously.)

Known only as Mrs Ward, a clergyman's widow, Horatia lived for some years at Elmdene, Church Lane, Pinner (centre). The photograph dates from about 1892.

Nelson himself concocted a highly transparent story in which Horatia became the daughter of a fellow seaman aboard HMS *Victory*, a man called Thompson or Thomson (since Nelson was rarely consistent in its spelling). To make matters even more complicated, on the day of his death at Trafalgar, Nelson wrote in his pocket-book that he left 'to the beneficence of my country, my adopted daughter, Horatia Nelson Thompson'.

A late nineteenth-century view of the Queen's Head Hotel, outside which Nelson's granddaughter met her death under the hooves of a bolting horse.

Years later, after Lady Hamilton had died in comparative poverty, the young Horatia petitioned the government of the day in the hope that they would honour her father's dying promise by providing her with an annual pension. Although Prime Minister William Canning proved sympathetic, he died unexpectedly before he could advance her claims. Horatia then sent all the documents of her case to his successor, Viscount Goderich (who, as recorded on p. 78, was one of seven Harrow-educated premiers). But Goderich's office merely returned them with a curt note to the effect that 'the great pressure of public business will prevent His Lordship from immediately taking into consideration your letter'.

At this point, Horatia, by now living with her father's relatives in Norfolk, seems to have decided to forget the past, a course in which she was greatly aided by a chance meeting with a young curate, the Revd Philip Ward. They were married in 1822 and, for many years to come, Horatia was only too pleased to be known simply as Mrs Ward, wife of the Vicar of Tenderden, Kent, and mother of a sizeable family. This included a son, Nelson, after his grandfather.

When Mr Ward died in 1839, it was only natural that Horatia would move in with her son, then living at West House in West End Lane. Subsequently, she moved to New House (now Elmdene) in Church Lane and, later still, to a villa on the same Woodridings Estate in Hatch End that was once home to the celebrated cook, Mrs Beeton. Throughout this period, she seems to have been known only as Ward's widow; indeed, the security of this new identity was convincingly demonstrated when another sadness befell the family.

On a summer Saturday in 1872, Ellen, a grown-up daughter, still living at home, was walking down Pinner High Street. British summers being much the same then as now, she was holding up an umbrella, which seems to have prevented her from seeing a runaway horse. As the *Harrow Gazette* reported at the time: 'Not noticing the horse coming,

This simple flat stone marks Horatia's Paines Lane cemetery grave.

she was knocked down and much trampled upon. Aid was immediately offered but she died at once and was taken into the Queen's Head.'

Significantly, the report gives only the name, Miss Ward of Woodridings, and makes no reference to her family, presumably because few, if any, local residents knew the family's true story.

Mrs Horatia Ward herself died in March 1881 and, today, her tombstone can readily be found in Paines Lane Cemetery. Yet, even in death, some element of confusion still remains. The tombstone proudly proclaims her 'the beloved daughter of Vice Admiral Lord Nelson'. But visitors will look in vain for any mention of her mother.

The Odeons

Though it no longer shows films, the Odeon at Rayners Lane is today a listed building.

At a time when Harrow's cinema-goers have to travel quite a way to find an Odeon Cinema – Kensington or Swiss Cottage are probably the nearest – it may be hard to imagine an era in which there was invariably an Odeon slap in the middle of a great many of our shopping parades.

Harrow in the 1940s, for example, could claim at least eight within easy travelling distance, at South Harrow, Kenton, Wealdstone, Sudbury Town, Kingsbury, Wembley, Colindale and Rayners Lane, although the latter had originally been built by the famous local firm of T.E. Nash, under the name of the Grosvenor.

Scholars will tell you that, ever since the days of Ancient Greece, the word Odeon (or odeum) has been used to describe a place for public performances. Nevertheless the circuit's founder, Oscar Deutsch, almost certainly chose the name because its first two letters were his own initials; indeed, his publicists subsequently claimed that Odeon actually stood for Oscar Deutsch Entertains Our Nation!

This was certainly no idle boast, especially in the grim days of the Second World War when the cinema was one of the very few entertainments, together with radio, that was available to all. In little more than a decade between the opening of his first cinema in 1930 and his tragically early death from cancer in 1941, Oscar Deutsch opened no fewer than 258 Odeons throughout Britain, more than half of them in brand-new, custom-designed buildings.

Deutsch, the Birmingham-born son of a Jewish-Hungarian scrap merchant, put up his very first Odeon sign in the Birmingham suburb of Perry Barr. At a time when so-called 'picture palaces' invariably took their inspiration from real-life palaces, this one was apparently modelled on some exotic Moroccan building. But Deutsch was already looking for something 'different'.

Soon, with the gifted A.P. Starkey as his principal architect, Deutsch began to give the world what quickly became known as 'the Odeon look' – a streamlined, modernist style whose exteriors frequently featured acres of gleaming white tiles.

At South Harrow, where the look was pioneered in 1936, the whole block between Scarsdale and Wyvenhoe Roads was given the same distinctive treatment, embracing not just the cinema but flats on either side as well as shops and an Odeon Café. The overall impact, according to a contemporary report, was 'like an ocean liner that had berthed inexplicably in a suburban High Street'.

Today, some thirty years after the cinema's closure, the left and right wings still remain virtually as built, with a large and somewhat incongruous apartment block in between.

To see what an Odeon really looked like in its 1930s heyday, you need to travel to Rayners Lane, where almost opposite the tube station (itself another monument to 1930s excellence) you will find the old Grosvenor/Odeon cinema which, as some rather crude lettering proclaims, is now used as a Zoroastrian Centre. But this recent lettering apart, the exterior is still virtually as it was when first designed by F.E. Bromige, complete with a towering glass wall, several storeys high, and a vast elephant trunk-style decoration that curves all the way from the roof down to the entrance canopy.

Behind the entrance doors, Bromige set a sunken Art Deco-syle restaurant, of which I have particularly fond memories as a child; not so much for its tea-time treats as for the glimpses it afforded of the cinema screen every time the auditorium's double doors opened – and, in those days of continuous performances, members of the audience were constantly on the move. (Hard as it may be for younger filmgoers to believe, you normally came out at the precise moment of the film at which you came in. Alternatively, you could always sit tight and see a favourite sequence again!)

It's 1957 and the end of an era for Sudbury Odeon, originally built as the centrepiece of an apartment/retail shopping block.

Bromige, it is worth recalling, produced an equally dazzling façade when called upon to design the Dominion (now The Safari) in Station Road, Harrow.

Sadly, in the 1960s, someone, presumably in the interests of modernity, took it upon themselves to cover up the entire frontage with some particularly undistinguished blue cladding, which remains to this day. However, it is good to note that this cinema has actually survived into the twenty-first century whereas, without exception, all of the immediately local Odeons ultimately fell victim, one by one, to the public's increasing addiction to television.

In today's South Harrow, all that remains of the once-popular Odeon is the tiled-faced block (left) and a companion block on the further side.

Faced with declining audiences, Kenton Odeon became a supermarket as long ago as 1961, the same year that Wealdstone Odeon also shut its doors, after which the building rotted away for at least a decade before the demolition men moved in. South Harrow survived until 1972, while Rayners Lane managed to achieve a fiftieth anniversary in 1986 (at which time the pre-war prices of 1s for the stalls and 2s for the circle were reinstated for a few special performances). But this too closed as a cinema that same year, although its Grade II listing ensured its survival as a building, run for some years as a so-called Cine-Bar Experience.

With hindsight, all the local Odeons, not to mention their many contemporaries, were just too big to survive. South Harrow was virtually a 1,000-seater and Kenton just 4 seats short of 1,400; these were giant capacities when compared with the 100–200-seat auditoria found in many of today's multi-screen buildings.

Prime Ministers

Sir Robert Peel, one of seven British prime ministers who received their education at Harrow School.

Given that Perceval, Peel and Palmerston all rose to the premiership of our land – and were all educated at Harrow School – they undoubtedly make a highly appropriate choice for our sixteenth alphabet entry.

Of the three, Spencer Perceval is perhaps the least well-known; yet his story is uniquely fascinating in that he was the first (indeed, the only) British prime minister to be assassinated in office. The assassination happened on Monday 11 May 1812, when John Bellingham, a bankrupt of disordered mind, stepped out from behind a pillar in the lobby of the House of Commons, placed a pistol at Perceval's heart and fired. Perceval was dead even before a doctor could

Spencer Perceval, Harrow School's first prime minister, who died from an assassin's bullet while attending the House of Commons.

be found. Not surprisingly, the manner of his death caused an universal outcry and the *Gentleman's Magazine* was comparatively restrained in commenting: 'It is with the deepest regret that we sully our pages by recording one of those atrocious events which to the honour of the British nation rarely occurs.'

Spencer Perceval entered Harrow School in 1774 and, like Winston Churchill in later years, does not seem to have been an especially industrious scholar. A letter from his father, the Earl of Egmont, states that 'from your mother's account of the heat in which she twice found you, I fear that football is upon the whole a more favourable pursuit with you than your books'. Nevertheless, by 1799, he had become a Monitor and, once he had reached Trinity College, Cambridge, his talents as a speaker were such that he gained the College Declamation Prize.

Perceval subsequently trained as a lawyer and, on entering Parliament, became successively Solicitor General (1801) and Attorney General (1802–4). Assuming the Premiership in December 1809, he had been in office little more than two years when his assassin struck.

At the time, he had young sons at Harrow School, one of whom was about to give a speech at an important school ceremony. The school's archives still retain the original programme of the event on which an unknown hand has written 'Not spoken in consequence of the assassination of his father'.

Tradition also has it that the three boys shown in a memorial to school founder, John Lyon, at St Mary's, Harrow on the Hill, were modelled on Perceval's sons: a not unreasonable supposition given that the monument (by the famous sculptor John Flaxman) was actually erected in the year of his death.

By 1834, the country again had an Old Harrovian prime minister in Sir Robert Peel, who had been a contemporary of Lord Byron at Harrow in the early nineteenth century. The two were not just schoolfellows but virtually birthday 'twins', Byron having been born on 22 January and Peel on 5 February of the year 1788. Nevertheless the oft-told Harrow tale of a sympathetic Byron endeavouring to take half a thrashing meted out to Peel is almost certainly apocryphal, given the fact that Byron came to the school almost a year after his friend-to-be.

The thrashing, however, was real enough and seems to have come about when Peel refused to fag for older boys. This incident apart, Peel appears to have been such a model schoolboy that Byron was later to remark, somewhat ruefully: 'There were always great hopes of Peel among us all, masters and scholars, and he has not disappointed them. As a scholar, he was greatly my superior; as a declaimer and actor, I was

As a means of increasing sales, this engraving of the Head Master's House following the fire of 1836 carries a personal dedication to Sir Robert Peel.

considered at least his equal; as a schoolboy out of school, I was always in scrapes and he never; and, in school, he always knew his lessons and I rarely.'

During his schooldays, Peel lived in the house of the Revd Mark Drury, which occupied High Street premises roughly where Moretons and the adjoining shop stand today and where, as many nineteenth-century reminiscences testify, he inscribed his name on a brick, now lost but apparently kept for many long years by an admiring school.

Even though his father, the former Member for Tamworth, bought him the seat of Cashel in Tipperary, Peel's very real abilities were to bring him the highest honours. He achieved the premiership twice (the second time in 1841). Today, however, he is probably best remembered for the creation of the Metropolitan Police Force during his time as Home Secretary. Bobby Peel, in fact, was so closely associated with the force that, for most of the last century, policeman were colloquially known as 'Bobbies'. Earlier still, of course, they had been nicknamed 'Peelers'.

By the 1850s Harrow School had the distinction of providing the country with two prime ministers in succession, the Stanmore-based Marquess of Aberdeen being immediately followed by Lord Palmerston.

As Henry John Temple, the name which can still be seen carved into the wooden panels of the school's Fourth Form Room, Palmerston was at Harrow from May 1794 in the house that ultimately became Druries but which was then kept by Dr Bromley. His grandfather, Benjamin Mee, had also been at the school, where he won the coveted Archery Prize.

Many accounts of young Temple's schooldays survive. In 1870, for example, Admiral Sir Augustus Clifford recalled being a fag to Althorp, Duncannon and Temple – 'and the latter was by far the most merciful and indulgent'. In common with other contemporaries, Clifford also recalls Temple fighting on the Milling Ground, a space specially kept for the pugilistic settlement of disputes, then located between the present Druries and the Bill Yard in front of Old Schools. On this occasion, Clifford says Temple's opponent was 'a great boy called Salisbury, twice his size and he [Temple] would not give in, but was brought home with black eyes and a bloody nose'.

During the summer vacation of 1799, Temple, in company with a younger brother who had joined him at the school, was taken on a visit to the House of Commons which, as he later claimed, inspired a political career during which he sat in no fewer than sixteen Parliaments. As Lord Palmerston, he was twice prime minister, from 1855 to 1858 and from 1859 to 1865. Throughout these years he was a familiar visitor to Harrow, winning the particular admiration of the townsfolk by his invariable custom of travelling on horseback, even in relatively old age and frequently in defiance of the weather.

Lord Palmerston, a frequent visitor to Harrow, invariably arriving on horseback.

One such occasion was in July 1861 when he laid the foundation stone of the school's Vaughan Library. According to the press of the day, he performed his duties 'with ample ceremony but less socialising than might have been expected': a polite way of saying that he left the town without partaking of the luncheon provided for distinguished guests. At this distance in time, we can only guess at the circumstances prompting his early departure. But, as our 'V' for Vaughan explains (pp. 103–8), it seems unlikely that Palmerston could have been aware

When in the late twentieth century Harrow headmasters wished to live apart from their pupils, a new private residence was built and named Peel House.

of the true story of Vaughan's sudden retirement: otherwise, as prime minister, he would probably have deemed it inappropriate to make any kind of appearance, no matter how brief.

More likely is the explanation that he was then engaged in a feud with the library's designer, George Gilbert Scott, having recently – and somewhat brusquely – rejected the latter's designs for a new India Office.

Yet another of Palmerston's visits to Harrow is amusingly recalled in J. Cotton Minchin's book *Old Harrow Days*. The occasion was Speech Day and, as usual, Palmerston rode down from London. Again, according to custom, he left his horse at the King's Head Stables, then walked the short distance to the Head Master's House in the High Street. He had, however, signally failed to notice how dirty and dishevelled he had become en route – so much so that when he presented himself at the head's house, he was initially refused admittance!

In a piece about Harrow prime ministers, it should perhaps be added that, over the years, Harrow School has educated a further four: the previously mentioned Lord Aberdeen and Sir Winston Churchill, as well as the long-forgotten Viscount Goderich, and Stanley Baldwin who, as premier on three separate occasions, virtually dominated the British political scene from 1923 to 1937.

It seems – and is – an impressive record for any school, until one recalls that Harrow's great rival, Eton, can lay claim to no fewer than eighteen old boys who have achieved Britain's highest political office.

Queen Adelaide

Queen Adelaide, wife of William IV, is the only monarch in history to have lived and died in Harrow.

Since the seventeenth letter of the alphabet stands for both queen and question, here's a little teaser for your next pub or party quiz. Which Queen of England not only lived within our borough but actually died there? The answer is the German-born Queen Adelaide, wife – and, by the time she reached Harrow, widow – of King William IV, whose brief reign (1830–7) came immediately before that of Queen Victoria.

Adelaide's journey to her final home, the great Stanmore mansion of Bentley Priory, was a long and rather sad one. Far from being a love match, her marriage in 1818 to William, then Duke of Clarence, had been arranged solely to protect the succession since his brother, the reigning King George IV, had lost his only child at birth. Adelaide was 26 at her wedding, her groom almost 30 years her senior.

Like many a queen before her (think especially of Anne Boleyn), Adelaide proved unable to produce the required male heir, though it was evidently not for want of trying. Between 1818 and 1824 she gave birth five times but all her babies were either stillborn or died in their very first year. (William's brother Edward, who was similarly hustled into marriage, fared rather better, his union producing one daughter, the future Queen Victoria.)

The cruellest irony was added to Adelaide's situation by the fact that William was widely known to have fathered ten illegitimate children by the actress Dorothea Jordan. This lady had also amassed considerable riches from her career, prompting an anonymous satirist to remark:

> As Jordan's high and mighty squire
> her playhouse profits deigns to skim,
> some folks audaciously enquire
> if he keeps her – or she keeps him.

When George IV died in 1830, Adelaide became queen but, since her husband was already 65 on his accession, she was to wear the crown for only seven years. Thus, in 1837 England found itself with its first dowager queen since the days of Catherine of Braganza and, earlier, Catherine Parr, respectively the widows of Charles II and Henry VIII.

However, whereas Braganza returned to Europe and Parr remarried, Adelaide stayed unattached – and in England. There being no precedent for such a situation, the government of the day decided to give her a state pension of £100,000 a year, which certainly freed her from financial worries. But where to live?

The first choice was Cassiobury, near Watford, where she remained for three years, during which time Watford railway station was

remodelled to give her a royal waiting room on her travels to London. But, since the Grand Junction Canal passed through the grounds of her mansion, her advisers felt that Cassiobury lacked sufficient privacy.

After a spell in Madeira for her declining health, Adelaide settled on Bentley Priory with the full approval of her doctors who remarked on Stanmore's 'salubrious air'. Even so, the dowager queen moved only into the ground-floor apartments to save her the effort of climbing its many grand staircases.

A devout as well as a modest woman, she would frequently attend services at the old St John's Church, Stanmore (to which she donated a font), but would always choose a seat at the back so that her now-persistent cough would not disturb the rest of the congregation.

Her invariable sweetness of nature seems to have endeared her to everyone in the district: certainly, Rimmer's 1882 book *Rambles around Eton and Harrow* states that many old people in the neighbourhood constantly spoke of her kindness and general love for everyone about her. And this verdict was amply endorsed in the letters of Queen Victoria who, in 1848, combined a visit to her bedside with an official visit to Harrow School.

In March 1849, Queen Adelaide made what was to be her last-ever public appearance at the ceremony to mark the laying of the foundation

In 1849 Queen Adelaide attended the laying of the foundation stone of St John's, Stanmore. It was to prove her last public appearance.

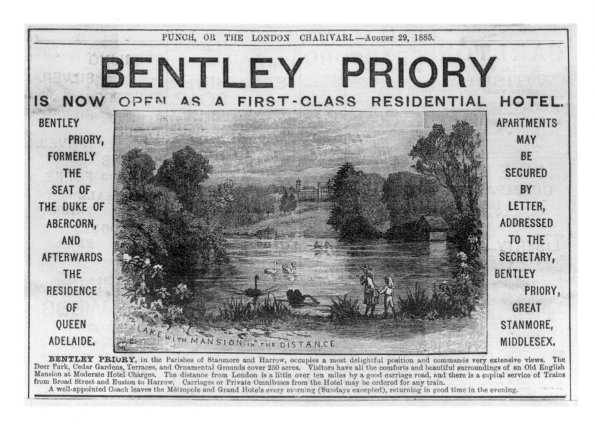

Once Bentley Priory had become an hotel, its advertising made much of its former royal connections.

stone of the present St John's Church in the grounds of the old. Nine months later, she was dead – at just 57. Modest to the end, Adelaide left instructions that her funeral was 'to give as little trouble as possible'. Nevertheless all of Stanmore seems to have turned out to pay its respects and, as the funeral cortège passed through Harrow on its way to Windsor, it was followed for much of the way by boys and masters of Harrow School.

As for her home at Bentley Priory, an astute businessman called Frederick Gordon acquired it some six years later and promptly turned it into an hotel. Inevitably, he made much of its royal connections, even featuring Adelaide's favourite garden summerhouse in his brochure. He also created a so-called Adelaide's room on an upper floor, cheerfully ignoring the fact that her quarters had always been downstairs and were currently being used as the hotel's kitchens.

Although today's Harrow Borough has long since forgotten its only resident monarch, her name is still perpetuated on the far side of the world, in the great South Australian city of Adelaide. Here, to this day, her statue remains in pride of place within the city's Town Hall.

Roxeth

Roxeth's controversial gas-holder dominated the local scene for over half a century.

Once you have realised that this entry for the letter 'R' concerns south Harrow, you may be forgiven for thinking I have muddled up the alphabet. But, in writing about south Harrow, I am simply using its old name of Roxeth ('good old Roxey'), which can be found in print as early as AD 845.

Roxeth is, admittedly, an odd-sounding name and nobody is absolutely sure of its origins. Some claim that it is a derivation of Rooks Heath (which is today the name of a large local school) and others that it refers to land belonging to an early British chieftain called Hroc.

As a name, however, south Harrow is indisputably the creation of the railway, appearing in print for the first time in 1893 when the Ealing & South Harrow Railway Bill was laid before Parliament. Subsequently it was chosen as the name for the new station opened in Northolt Road in 1903. Incidentally, if you go just a few yards up South Hill Avenue, you can still see the original station house which, happily, survived a complete rebuilding of the station in the mid-1930s. As anticipated, the new line, the first direct route from Harrow to the Kensington museums and the West End shops, was a huge success, giving further impetus to the growth of a community that was already thriving in the nineteenth century.

Roxeth Gasworks was a Northolt Road landmark for much of the last century. Its decontaminated site now houses a supermarket.

In comparison with the neighbouring Harrow Hill, it was then seen as very much a working-class community and, in truth, a great many of its residents either worked directly or indirectly for Harrow School and its masters or were employed in the gasworks, which had opened in Northolt Road in 1855.

Roxeth from the air in 1922 reveals a concentration of buildings around the gasworks (centre) in an expanse of otherwise open land.

The man who first brought gas not just to Roxeth but to the whole area was a builder called John Chapman who, from its inception, had been a member of the Harrow Board of Health. So when the board advertised in *The Times* in May 1855 for a company to establish a public gas supply, Chapman was quick to accept the challenge, pledging to complete the job in just six months. He proved as good as his word and, by September of the same year, he was able to host a banquet in the King's Head Hotel (see pp. 51–6) at which cheers rang out as the hotel's new gas chandelier was lit for the very first time.

By the following year, the first street gas lighting was in place. These early lamps were lit manually and, by 1881, many complaints were being heard. Amusingly, they were not about the extent or the quality of the lighting but about the loud voice of the local lamp-lighter, one Alfred Dear, who would persist in singing on his twice-daily rounds!

Given their Sunday-best clothing here, Roxey residents were possibly en route to the Baptist Mission Tent set up in the fields of Grange Farm, *c.* 1905.

Earlier still, the Revd John Cunningham, realising that local children were no longer attending John Lyon's foundation, had opened a parochial school on Roxeth Hill. Decades later, he was to see this little establishment transformed into today's Roxeth First and Middle Schools after persuading the famous philanthropist Lord Shaftesbury to award his school the considerable sum collected as a memorial to Shaftesbury's son who had died while a Harrow School pupil. Cunningham had also wished to see a daughter church to St Mary's in the Roxeth area although, in the event, this did not arise until the year after his death. It was in the handsome guise of Christ Church, Roxeth Hill, to designs by George Gilbert Scott, who had already left a considerable architectural heritage on the hill.

Old Roxeth was also able to boast our town's very first hospitals (see pp. 37–42): originally two converted cottages on Roxeth Hill, then a small villa in Lower Road and, finally, the Harrow Cottage Hospital of 1906, which faithfully served the community for the better part of the twentieth century. It is sad but inevitable that this whole chapter in Roxeth's history will soon be as competely forgotten as the Great Barn of Roxeth, one of the finest of the old Middlesex barns, which dominated the Roxeth Corner end of Northolt Road until it was demolished just after the Second World War.

The people of Roxeth undoubtedly believed in pulling together and their community spirit won them in March 1898 one of the first recreation grounds in the district. Four years earlier, they had formed the Roxeth and Harrow Church Lads Brigade, now the oldest surviving youth organisation in the borough, while a citadel of the Salvation Army was opened at the foot of Roxeth Hill as early as 1886 (see p. 90).

If Roxey's residents worked hard, they also played hard and the district was very well supplied with drinking places of every description. Among them was the long-since-vanished Three Horseshoes (first licensed in 1730), the still-surviving Half Moon, originally dating from 1862, and its near neighbour the Timber Carriage, which, in an earlier and more modest incarnation, bore the more modest name of the Timber Truck! Roxeth even had its own immensely popular sports and amusement grounds known as The Paddocks, which were later absorbed into the present Alexandra Park.

As late as 1907, the area had nine licensed houses and four off-licences within a quarter of a mile. Among the earliest was the Half Moon at Roxeth Corner.

Roxeth's Cub Pack on open ground between what is now Wargrave Road (left) and Scarsdale Road (right) with Kingsley Road in the background, c. 1920.

In more recent times a blot (almost literally) appeared on the Roxeth landscape. This was the huge gas-holder which, amid great controversy, rose on the gasworks site in the early 1930s and remained in place, if not in use, right up to 1986. Stories about it abound. My personal (and well-authenticated) favourite concerns the pilot who, mistaking the holder for a similar one near Southall, put his plane down at nearby Northolt Airport rather than its proper destination of Heathrow.

In an attempt to ensure that such an incident never occurred again, a gigantic 'NO' was painted on the side of the gas-holder (see p. 83). However, I have never been able to establish whether this meant NO LANDING HERE or was simply short-hand for NORTHOLT. Either way, the device seems to have worked.

Salvation Army

Members of the Wealdstone Salvation Army seen outside the Palmerston Road Citadel, *c.* 1932.

If there is one national organisation about which one rarely, if ever, hears an unkind word, it has to be the Salvation Army. This is all the more amazing when one recollects the atmosphere of resentment, indeed, of downright hostility, in which William Booth founded his unique organisation in 1878.

The Nottingham-born Booth, who was taken away from school at 13 and apprenticed to a pawnbroker, obviously knew at first hand how tough the world could be for the poor. But even he must have been shocked and surprised by the cruelty and vindictiveness with which his efforts to improve their lot were initially subjected.

Hardly a meeting took place at which he and his supporters were not subjected to both physical and verbal abuse, but this only hardened Booth's resolve. When they were deluged with spit on a Midlands tour, he told his fellow officers, 'Don't rub it off – it's a medal'.

As it happened, even the good people of relatively genteel Harrow were more than a little hesitant in their acceptance of the Army when it first moved to Wealdstone in the 1880s.

Since a lot of the Army's records were lost in the Blitz of the Second World War, it is now impossible to say precisely why, before the decade was out, the early Salvationists decided to open a second mission in the district, choosing a site at Roxeth Corner, where Northolt Road meets Roxeth Hill. They may have been influenced by the poverty then rife in an area which, as you can read under R for Roxeth, was largely dependent for its work and patronage on its wealthier neighbours. Then, too, they could have been encouraged by the presence on the hill of a few philanthropic souls, among them the boys' adventure writer, R.M. Ballantyne. After years abroad, Ballantyne had just acquired Duneaves on the Mount Park Estate where General Booth himself is known to have been an early visitor.

Whatever the reason for the Army's arrival on Roxeth Hill in December 1886, the local paper, then the *Harrow Gazette*, was distinctly sniffy about the whole venture. Although honesty compelled them to admit that there had been no 'unruliness'at the opening, they could not resist describing the audience as 'about one hundred of the roughest element'.

There were also doubts about the safety of these first premises, an upper room in what had once been Mr Card's shed for which the only entrance and exit was provided by a step-ladder. As for the meeting room itself, it was heated by a stove and lit by ten oil lamps hanging from the walls. So, despite the suspicions of certain Army supporters, the decision of the Local Board of Health to insist upon frequent inspections was to protect rather than to harass them.

The Roxeth Citadel's opening day was marked by heavy snowfalls. This was undeniably fatiguing for the marchers and, in a rare moment of sympathy, the writer of the press report was moved to add: 'We can understand the exclamation of one of the musicians who, on leaving the town in the evening, said . . . they had had a terrible battle with the Devil that day.'

Local road workers, photographed in the early 1920s, were among the groups to which the first Salvationists appealed.

The 'battle', however, proved one well worth fighting and, by 1906, attitudes to the Salvation Army had changed so dramatically that the Liberal Member of Parliament for the Harrow Division, James Gibb, consented to lay the foundation stone for a new citadel, again on Roxeth Hill. Seating some 400 and built at a cost of around £1,600 (of which at least half was raised by the local Corps), the new building had a suitably proud opening by a former High Sheriff of the County.

From the very earliest days, both the Roxeth and Wealdstone Corps put great faith – in every sense of the word – in the persuasive powers of music, always remembering that General Booth himself believed that God (not the Devil) should have 'all the best tunes'. Nevertheless one cannot help but speculate on the comments of the seriously ill when, according to a 1907 press report, the Band visited the very new Harrow Cottage Hospital and treated them to 'several verses of the hymn, Nearer My God To Thee'.

In summer 2004, the Roxeth Hill Citadel, much of which is almost 100 years old, awaits redevelopment.

For the most part, however, there can be no denying that the Army's good intentions were invariably matched by their good results. To give only one example, as recorded by the Wealdstone historian, H.M. Wilkins, the Army provided breakfast for up to 50 poor children several mornings a week during the harsh winter of 1909. For just one farthing (a quarter of one old penny), they enjoyed both a bowl of porridge and a plate of bread and jam. And, true to the Army's tradition, even if the children didn't have a farthing they still got fed.

No wonder then that, by 1928, a 'Round the Churches' feature in the local press could comment: 'Probably no organisation has achieved such a great work among the type of people who seem out of reach of the churches.'

Decades later, local Salvation Army members were to the fore at the Wealdstone train disaster of October 1952, helping with the rescue work (which continued for days) and setting up a much appreciated rescuers' canteen.

In more recent times, the Harrow Corps on Roxeth Hill has become the single Salvation Army presence in the borough, and in the past 12 months alone has given not one but two concerts on Harrow Hill, both happily supported by all sections of the community.

In addition, as this book goes to press, it is fast developing plans for a brand-new building on the Roxeth Hill site in the hope that its twenty-first-century work can be every bit as productive as that accomplished during its first 117 years.

The Trollope Family

One of the Harrow homes of the famous literary family inspired this frontispiece illustration to Anthony Trollope's *Orley Farm*.

Without in any way seeking to diminish the status of those great Old Harrovians, Lord Byron and Richard Brinsley Sheridan, there can be no doubt that, as a family, it is the Trollopes who reign supreme in Harrow's literary Hall of Fame. It is not just that, 122 years after his death, Anthony Trollope remains one of our most popular storytellers, as the many TV adaptations of his work confirm. The literary reputation of Fanny, his mother, continues to rise year on year, while anyone seeking a richly entertaining record of the family's turbulent life in our midst need look no further than *What I Remember*, the reminiscences of his brother, Thomas.

Anthony Trollope (seen here in his later years) remains one of Britain's best-loved novelists. In addition, his work is constantly adapted for TV and radio.

That our town can lay claim to this amazing family is entirely owing to the head of the household, the lawyer Thomas Trollope. Fancying himself as a farmer, in 1813 Thomas moved from London to the then-rural Harrow where he negotiated a lease from Lord Northwick on a property called Illot's Farm, off today's Julian Hill on Harrow Hill.

Soon afterwards, he decided to build his own grand house on the land, gambling on the expectation of a substantial inheritance from a bachelor uncle. The house duly went up –it still stands today – but the anticipated money never materialised since the uncle not only made a late marriage but also produced an heir. Worse still, the farm was soon losing so much money that the only practical solution was for the Trollopes to let their fine new family home. It was ultimately taken by the the Revd John Cunningham, the Vicar of Harrow, a move which was to create reverberations that echo to this very day.

For a while, the family was obliged to split up. Anthony moved with his father to what he later described as a tumbledown farmhouse in Harrow Weald, from which he had to walk, sometimes twice daily, to Harrow School, much to the cruel amusement of his aristocratic schoolfellows.

As he wrote in his autobiography, this was 'the worst period in my life', in which nothing was more hateful than 'those dreadful walks, backwards and forwards . . . four times a day, in wet and dry, in heat and summer with all the accompanying mud and dust, and with disordered clothes. I might have been known by all the boys at 100 yards distance by my boots and trousers – and was conscious at times that I was so known'.

Nor could he find comfort (in any sense of the word) in his new Harrow Weald home – 'as it crept downwards from house to stables, stables to barn, from barn to cowshed and from cowshed to dung heap, one could hardly tell where one began and the other ended'.

Meanwhile his mother Fanny had sailed for the United States, quite an adventure in the 1820s, in the hope of restoring the family fortunes. But this was not quite as foolhardy as it seems. In 1823, Fanny Trollope had visited Paris and become friendly with the American Revolutionary hero General Lafayette, and his ward, Frances Wright, a lady who, as a personal experiment in abolitionism, had purchased an estate called Nashoba in Western Tennessee. It was to Nashoba that Fanny first came on arrival in America; indeed, the Nashoba estate actually loaned her $300 to help her first business enterprise, a bazaar selling English fancy goods in Cincinnati, Ohio.

Described as a kind of 'Arabian Nights edifice', the bazaar attracted interested comment rather than actual custom and did not survive for long. Undaunted, Fanny turned her hand to writing, putting her transatlantic experiences into a book called *The Domestic Manners of the Americans*, which not only proved a considerable if unexpected success but also launched her on a long and notable literary career.

More to the immediate point, its financial success enabled her to bring Anthony and the family back to the hill, though not to the great house but to the smaller farmhouse on the same site. The fact that Mr Cunningham still occupied what they undoubtedly saw as their

Fanny Trollope, Anthony's mother, belied her sweetly feminine looks with a steely ambition that took her to America – and on to literary fame.

The original mansion built for the Trollopes still survives as a family home on Harrow Hill.

family home obviously rankled with them and, in subsequent years, both mother and son were to pillory Cunningham in print.

Fanny's story about an unpleasant cleric, *The Vicar of Wrexhill*, was widely regarded as a portrait of Harrow's vicar. Even more damagingly, Anthony Trollope is said to have taken Cunningham as the model for the slippery Obadiah Slope in his 'Barchester Chronicles' series (which, as many will recall, once provided a memorable TV role for Alan Rickman). The story obviously lingers on, for only last year, the slope leading off the High Street to Harrow School's dining complex was officially christened Obadiah Slope!

From the farmhouse on Julian Hill, Anthony continued his Harrow education in 'somewhat improved circumstances'. 'The three miles', he later wrote, 'became half a mile and probably some salutary changes were made to my wardrobe.' But it was too late for him to change his opinion of life at Harrow. As his autobiography declares: 'I feel convinced in my mind that I have been flogged oftener than any human being alive'.

If school life was marginally more bearable, life with father continued full of surprises. One day, on driving his father in a horse-drawn gig to

London, he suddenly realised that Thomas Trollope's ultimate destination was the Ostend boat. As Trollope tells it, 'it was not in his nature to be communicative and to the last he never told me why he was going to Ostend'.

Once Anthony had returned to Julian Hill, the reason was all too apparent: his father was fleeing his creditors and the house was already full of the sheriff's men. Anthony had the presence of mind to drive straight into Harrow Town, where he sold the entire equipage to an ironmonger for £17. Predictably, Fanny was even more resourceful. As Anthony later wrote: 'my mother, through all her various troubles, had continued to keep a certain number of pretty-pretties which were dear to her heart . . . and these were being carried surreptitiously through a gap between the two gardens on to the premises of our friend Colonel Grant. My two sisters, then 16 and 17 and the Grant girls who were just younger, were the chief marauders. To such forces I was happy to add myself for any enterprise.'

If Trollope ever returned to the town which had caused him so much heartache, the fact has not been recorded. Nevertheless, many years later, by which time he had become one of the most successful novelists

Only drawings now remain of the Harrow Weald farm where Anthony was obliged to live when the family's fortunes collapsed.

of the day, he drew on memories of his boyhood for one of his most enduringly popular novels, *Orley Farm*. He also gave the well-known artist John Millais a detailed description of the kind of farm he wished to see illustrated as the novel's frontispiece (reproduced on p. 93). Though Millais felt artistically justified in adding a few rural touches of his own (such as the cow and milkmaid in the foreground), there is no denying that his picture is remarkably close to surviving photographs of the original farm.

Readers unfamiliar with the next sequence of events may already be wondering if there is any positive connection between the name of the novel and Harrow's long-established Orley Farm School. That the answer is a resounding 'Yes' stems from the quick-wittedness of one E.M. 'Teddy' Hastings who, at the instigation of his good friend Harrow Head Master Charles Vaughan, had earlier opened a small school where boys could be prepared for their subsequent education at Harrow itself.

Although this school began on Sudbury Hill, it had subsequently moved to Julian Hill, site of the Trollope homes. Imagine then Hastings' surprise on opening a newly bought copy of *Orley Farm* and seeing what appeared to be an extremely familiar building featured on its frontispiece.

Aware of its inherent publicity value, Hastings promptly obtained Trollope's permission not only to use the name Orley Farm for his school but also to feature the Millais drawing on its prospectus. It was, of course, under the name Orley Farm that the school moved in 1901 to elegant new premises designed by the distinguished Arnold Mitchell and where, much extended and improved, it remains to this very day.

University

One of many major buildings that now make up the impressive Harrow campus of the University of Westminster.

Thank heavens Harrow now has a university on its doorstep. Otherwise, this twenty-first entry in our alphabet might have been devoted to the borough's undertakers! Its name – the University of Westminster – is admittedly relatively new, dating only from 1992. But its predecessor bodies can trace their history right back to 1838 when Britain's first Polytechnic Institution opened in London's Regent Street so that 'the public, at little expense, may acquire . . . a practical knowledge of the various arts and branches of science'.

The original driving force was Sir George Cayley, a landowner and gentleman scientist, whose pioneering vision attracted the support of both Queen Victoria's consort, Prince Albert, and the Harrow School-educated William Fox Talbot who, in 1841, signed an agreement allowing the Polytechnic to demonstrate his new photographic process. Within months, the Polytechnic had opened Europe's first-ever photographic studio.

When Cayley died in 1857 the torch was taken up by Quintin Hogg, who set out to appeal directly to the thousands of young men and, from 1888, young women, whose lives and prospects could be enriched by the new 'technical education'.

At much the same time, similar ideas were being propounded on Harrow Hill, most notably by Marion Hewlett, who lived at Harrow House adjoining the King's Head Hotel.

Marion Hewlett, whose energy and resourcefulness was largely responsible for introducing 'technical education' to Harrow.

The Hewletts were a prime example of those comfortably off Victorian professional families who felt it their bounden duty to improve the lot of those less privileged. Marion's father was Thomas Hewlett, school and town doctor, who had already done much to modernise the town by such essential means as proper drainage and sanitation and two, at least, of his large family devoted themselves to progressive causes. Constance Hewlett battled for a local hospital service (see p. 38) while Marion Hewlett tackled the sad lack of education she witnessed all around her, especially among the many young people then employed in domestic service on the hill. Using local homes as a base, she started evening classes designed 'to develop among boys and girls higher ideals and love of art and science'.

Fortunately, these somewhat lofty sentiments did not preclude a healthy streak of practicality and right from the start there were cookery classes, Miss Hewlett evidently sharing Mrs Beeton's view that 'many working class homes are made miserable by bad cooking'. Miss Hewlett was equally convinced of the need for dressmaking classes. 'It is an undoubted fact,' she wrote, 'that, in London, thousands of French dressmakers are employed because English women cannot be found competent either to cut out dresses or to fit them correctly.'

Already confident of help from Harrow Hill notables – and with newly found premises at 100 High Street – Marion Hewlett sought to bolster her developing school with royal patronage. Accordingly, she approached Princess Louise, a daughter of Queen Victoria, who already shared her interest in the animal welfare group known as the Band of Mercy. Generously, the princess not only consented to become the school's patron but also agreed to visit the first exhibition of its class work.

This exhibition was duly held in May 1889 (when the schoolboy Winston Churchill was numbered among the visitor's guard of honour) and its very real success provided exactly the boost Miss Hewlett's educational campaign required. Indeed, within 12 years, the local newspaper was able to publish an architect's drawing of the new technical school 'now in course of construction on a site in Station Road, Greenhill'. Older readers will un-doubtedly recall with affection the handsome red-brick building that ultimately arose on a site not far from the junction with College Road and which, by 1910, already had some 500 young people on its register.

Under the somewhat cumbersome title of Harrow Technical College and School of Art, it continued to prosper, occasionally hitting the headlines through the success of past pupils. In 1981, in particular, the whole world seemed to know that the wedding dress of the Princess of Wales had been designed by David and Elizabeth Emanuel, who had met on the American-born Elizabeth's very first day at the college. Charlie Watts, drummer with the Rolling Stones, is another famous name on the registers.

By then, the old 'Tech' had moved to a new building on a 26-acre greenfield site at Northwick Park, the first phase of which was opened in 1961. Twelve years later, the college might well have been forced to

The schoolboy Winston Churchill – one of Harrow School's guard of honour when Marion Hewlett brought Queen Victoria's daughter to Harrow Hill.

A familiar landmark in Station Road for decades, the red-brick 'Tech' is seen shortly after its opening in 1901.

close had not 70 firemen from all over London successfully fought a fire in the roof of the pottery department which threatened to engulf other parts of the premises.

In 1988, students were able to mark the centenary of Marion Hewlett's first classes by taking a double-decker bus around the borough, enacting scenes from the college's first 100 years at various Harrow locations. Now known as the Harrow College of Higher Education, it was subsequently merged with the original Regent Street establishment, which in more recent times had become the Polytechnic of Central London.

When the two institutions were finally rededicated as the University of Westminster at a service in Westminster Abbey in December 1992, the Bishop of London, very properly, made much of the 'vision' of its founders. Nevertheless one doubts whether people such as Marion Hewlett, even at their most visionary, could ever have contemplated a place of education with the size and spread of today's university, or the scale and diversity of its curriculum.

Charles Vaughan

The Victorian
Charles Vaughan was
one of Harrow
School's most
charismatic and
controversial
headmasters.

By a happy coincidence, our letter 'V' can stand not just for Charles Vaughan, who gave his name to Harrow Hill's spectacular Vaughan Library, but also for Victorian, since this complex man in many ways enshrined both the best and the worst of the Victorian era.

The best is easily described. The second son of the Vicar of St Martin's, Leicester, Vaughan was a schoolboy at Rugby under the great Dr Arnold (of *Tom Brown's Schooldays* fame), and later a distinguished scholar at Cambridge. Although his initial studies were for the law, he subsequently decided to follow the calling of his father and elder brother and was duly ordained in 1841. Shortly afterwards, he was appointed to his father's old parish. His mentors, however, had more ambitious plans for him and, a year later, it was only the dissenting vote of one governor that prevented him from succeeding Arnold as headmaster of Rugby. Rugby's loss proved Harrow's gain. Within two years he had been offered and accepted its headmastership. Amazingly, he was still only in his late twenties.

Initially, this was to prove a far from easy role. Harrow was at a low ebb numerically; furthermore, discipline and morale were so poor that Harrow's influential vicar, the Revd John Cunningham, supposedly urged him to expel the whole school and to take back only boys of his

In August 1863 the *Illustrated London News* gave its readers this splendid drawing of the library built on Vaughan's resignation – but no inkling of the reason behind his departure.

own choosing. But Vaughan's charisma and determination were quickly instrumental in raising the school roll to around 200. By the mid-1850s, it had reached around 460.

During this period, Vaughan added new boarding houses and a new chapel. He even extended the playing fields, winning a widespread reputation as Harrow's 'second founder'. He also found an ingenious solution to the perennial complaint that, in becoming a school for the aristocracy, Harrow had betrayed John Lyon's original intention of providing grammar school education for local boys.

In 1853, Vaughan – out of his own pocket and against the wishes of the governors – opened an 'English school of commercial character' where the sons of local farmers and tradesmen were taught relevant subjects in their own language (unlike the main school curriculum which was then largely taught in Latin). This, in turn, paved the way for the creation in 1876 of the Lower School of John Lyon, today's much respected John Lyon School.

Though it was widely accepted that so brilliant a man would not stay at Harrow indefinitely – he was even talked of as a future archbishop of Canterbury – the educational world was shattered when, after just 15 years, the 45-year-old Vaughan suddenly announced his resignation.

The prime minister, Lord Palmerston, himself an Old Harrovian, promptly offered him the Bishopric of Worcester but this was politely declined. According to the 1899 edition of the *Dictionary of National*

Now completely modernised and computerised, the library once housed not only books but also many of the school's pictures and other treasures.

The present-day John Lyon School originated with the 'English Form', which Vaughan not only founded but also funded from his own pocket.

Biography, 'A few months later, Lord Palmerston . . . offered him the See of Rochester. He accepted without hesitation. A day or two later, probably after a severe struggle with his ambition, the acceptance was withdrawn.'

It was, in truth, a severe struggle that Vaughan faced, though at its heart lay impropriety rather than ambition. What Palmerston evidently did not know – a secret held by only the merest handful of people – was that Vaughan had been accused of behaving improperly with one of his pupils, Alfred Pretor. This came to light belatedly through the apparent jealousy of another pupil, John Addington Symonds, to whom Pretor had foolishly, and perhaps boastfully, written of the affair. When Symonds expressed doubts, Pretor showed him a series of incriminating letters that had passed between headmaster and pupil.

Symonds did nothing for some years but, while at university, confided the whole story to one John Conington. Suitably horrified, Conington insisted that Symonds tell his father, and Dr Symonds promptly wrote to Vaughan, making it abundantly plain that resignation was the only possible alternative to exposure. Even more harshly, Symonds insisted that Vaughan henceforth decline any role of real influence, in the Church or elsewhere.

Despite the tearful pleadings of Mrs Vaughan, who was the daughter of the Bishop of Norwich, Dr Symonds remained adamant and Vaughan duly announced his resignation. He was, in fact, hard put to find a convincing argument for his departure, contenting himself with the remark – given at a farewell banquet – that '15 years of headmastership was as much as a man's strength could stand and quite enough for the welfare of the school he governed'.

It is here that an element of typical Victorian hypocrisy enters the story, for each time Vaughan turned down some high office his reputation for integrity, even sanctity, increased. However, his offer to prepare graduates of any university for the ministry was accepted.

It is interesting – if ultimately pointless – to speculate just how many people at Harrow knew the real reason for Vaughan's resignation. Certainly, the school went ahead with a plan to build a magnificent Library in his name and Lord Palmerston (see pp. 77–8) even came to Harrow to lay its foundation stone. But there was no major ceremony for its opening.

Significantly, certain contemporary commentators were cautious in their written assessments of Vaughan. For example, J. Cotton Minchin, in his *Old Harrow Days*, published in 1898, a year after Charles Vaughan's death, wrote: 'Dr. Vaughan seems to have been more a

George Gilbert Scott, architect of the Albert Memorial, gave Harrow some of its finest buildings, including the library (right) and the school chapel (left).

A later drawing of Charles Vaughan marking his acceptance of the Mastership of the Temple in 1869.

favourite with the boys than the masters. Dr. Butler [Vaughan's successor] always spoke of him with unbounded enthusiasm but this one would expect from so warm-hearted a man . . . I have rarely heard any other master refer to him.'

How did the whole sorry story finally come to light? After all, Vaughan ordered that all his letters be destroyed on his death and, more particularly, was insistent that no biography ever be written – a request that has been honoured to this day. John Addington Symonds' papers, however, survived him. And in recent years a more relaxed climate has permitted the publication of details that previous generations had felt unsuitable for the public gaze.

It should perhaps be added that Symonds himself had a not undistinguished career as an art historian. A chronic chest infection, however, saw him settle in Davos in Switzerland where he is said to have intimately involved himself in every aspect of the local community. In this context, as I wrote in my earlier *Book of Harrow on the Hill*, one cannot help but wonder if his entry in the 1898 *Dictionary of National Biography* is quite as innocuous as it first appears: 'Notwithstanding his habitual association with men of the highest culture, no trait in his character was more marked than his readiness to fraternise with peasant and artisan.'

Watkin's Tower

One of the winning designs for Britain's Eiffel Tower reproduced in a June 1890 magazine.

FIG. 1.—FIRST PRIZE.

At first glance, Sir Edward Watkin may seem an obscure choice to represent 'W' in this *Harrow A to Z*. Yet had his dreams been fulfilled, everyone would know his name in exactly the same way and, indeed, for exactly the same reason that we now acknowledge France's Gustav Eiffel. Watkin's dream was to erect the tallest structure in the world, just across our borders in Wembley. But sadly, what began as Watkin's Tower ended its days as Watkin's Folly.

The inspiration for this vast and expensive project was, of course, the Eiffel Tower, especially the fact that in seven short months its promoters had managed to recover the entire cost of its construction. Sir Edward, then chairman of the Metropolitan Railway, argued that a similar tower built somewhere along his company's line would become not only a considerable money-maker in its own right but would also boost the

Watkin's Tower was meant to rival the Eiffel Tower yet never rose beyond this 190ft platform. Later, its grounds became an amusement park entered by the ornamental gates.

railway's traffic. As a result, the summer of 1890 witnessed his acquisition of some 280 acres at Wembley Park where the 'Met' set about building a new railway station.

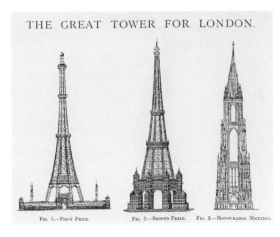

THE GREAT TOWER FOR LONDON.

Fig. 1.—First Prize.   Fig. 2.—Second Prize.   Fig. 3.—Honourable Mention.

The three winning designs for Britain's Eiffel Tower were reproduced in a June 1890 magazine.

To capitalise on the tower's publicity value, Watkins astutely announced an international design competition offering generous prizes of 500 guineas and 250 guineas for a structure which, according to the competition rules, had to be not less than 1,200ft high – that is, some 300ft taller than the Eiffel Tower.

The response could hardly have been more encouraging. Some 68 designs were received not only from all parts of Britain but also from Europe, the Middle East, the United States, Canada and Australia.

They were, as our illustrations reveal, highly imaginative if not always entirely practical, one Australian entrant even submitting a tower on giant wheels which, he claimed, could easily be towed by ship across the seabed. It could be recommended, he said, 'for obviating the terrors of sickness on the Channel passage until such time as the Channel tunnel may have become an established fact'.

Although the entries created considerable excitement at a special exhibition in the City of London, the judges did not consider any single design wholly suitable. So, when building work finally began, it was on an amalgam of entries more or less patched together by Sir Benjamin Baker, designer of the Forth Bridge. Faced with plans that called for an hotel, a theatre, shops, Turkish baths and an observatory, Baker sensibly brought in many of the men who had worked with him on the earlier project.

Initially, work went smoothly enough and, by 1893, the *Harrow Gazette* was enthusing about the structure 'beginning to peep over the tree-tops' to which, they prophesied, 'the public will eventually flock in thousands'. Some two years later, the same paper was able to report the completion of the first stage, 'which consists of a gigantic platform 190–200ft from the ground'. But already the seeds of doubt were beginning to be sown for, in commenting on the proposed 90-bed hotel, the paper somewhat sniffily declared: 'Whether this is likely to be carried out at present we are not informed.'

In fact, the first platform – which alone utilised some 2,700 tons of steel – was to prove the summit of the builders' achievement.

Since the tower's grounds were, by now, handsomely landscaped (and Watkins had completed a convenient station at Wembley Park), the decision was taken to open the partially built tower as a tourist attraction. But the anticipated crowds failed to materialise: some said because the railway fare to Wembley was too high; others that the vista from the partially built tower (in reality, over the fairly empty Wembley countryside) could hardly compare with the views of Paris obtained from the Eiffel Tower.

Thus, when Sir Edward himself fell ill and died, the promoters found it impossible to raise sufficient funds for the continuance of the scheme, especially as the most recent soil survey had cast some doubt on the likelihood of Middlesex clay ever being able to support so heavy a load. Anxious to save something from the mess, the tower company now reformed itself as the Wembley Park Estate Company and set about developing the land for housing.

To this end, in 1907, work began on removing the tower which the press was now describing as an 'unsightly blot on the landscape'. Dismantling so heavy a structure was, inevitably a long and difficult procedure, and even cost the life of one young workman who was struck by a falling girder. Finally, all that remained of Watkin's dream was blown up in a carefully controlled explosion.

The (very literal) fall of the tower left several unanswered questions, notably whether the scheme truly died with its creator – or whether Watkin, with his renowned financial acumen and powers of persuasion,

Within 20 years of the tower's demolition, Watkin's dream of Wembley as a tourist attraction was realised with the creation of the vast British Empire Exhibition.

could ever have won sufficient money and support for its completion.

Almost one hundred years on, these are impossible questions to answer. But one crucial point should be made in Watkin's favour. Had his tower reached its full height, it would have dominated the landscape from a point right in the middle of what, just a few decades later, became Wembley Stadium. And that, as the whole world knows, rarely failed to attract the crowds – as, it is hoped, will the new stadium currently rising on the very same site.

X Certificate

Ten Nights in a Bar Room, showing here at the Wealdstone Coronet, was the kind of catchpenny film which brought about the first censorship.

When the original version of this A to Z first appeared in the *Harrow Observer*, the immediate response of many readers was 'What will you do for X?' After all, Harrow is not exactly noted for discoveries in X-ray technology, nor indeed the talents of its xylophone players!

Inevitably, the answer has to be a little bit of a cheat. Our chosen theme is, in fact, cinema censorship or, more specifically, the X certificate which, for decades, was the film classification that stopped cinemagoers under 18 being exposed to what were considered 'unsuitable' films. 'Suitability', of course, has had a very different meaning for different generations. Over 70 years ago, Harrow's Medical Officer of Health, Charles E. Goddard, felt so strongly on the matter that he used his 1930 Annual Report to the then Urban District Council as a vehicle for a strongly worded warning against what he saw as 'a very great evil that is taking place in our midst'.

Sandwiched between the expected statistics on infectious diseases and mortality rates, Goddard used a substantial section of his report to affirm his belief that the cinema was doing a positive injury to 'the moral and mental health of the people'. He was especially contemptuous of American films. 'These performances', he declared, 'are often full of suggestive, adulterous matter, bedroom scenes, intemperance, dancing on supper tables, young women apparently of the prostitute type embracing elderly men; they include scenes of violence, debauchery, even murder, and are always full of strong sexual appeal.'

Though his choice of targets (table-dancing?) seems fairly risible to us today, it is a fact that US films of the early 1930s were a good deal raunchier than their successors, for a certain Will Hays had yet to force through the self-censoring Production Code which quickly placed film-makers in a kind of moral strait-jacket. The code was grudgingly accepted by an industry racked with scandals such as the Fatty Arbuckle murder case, but it outraged liberals like the writer Gene Fowler who mockingly declared, 'Will Hays is my shepherd. He maketh me lie down in clean postures.'

Even as Charles Goddard was writing, the British industry had an additional safeguard in its own post-production self-censoring body, the BBFC (which, then as now, actually charged film-makers for its services). Today the 'FC' part of its title no longer stands for Film Censorship (since censorship itself has become something of a dirty word in many quarters) but for Film Classification.

Not surprisingly, the classifications themselves have changed over the years. In the less permissive period prior to the Second World War, films were either H for Horror, U for Universal or A for Adult. Children, however, could attend an A feature if accompanied by an

adult, not necessarily even someone they knew. (How many of us, I wonder, have at some time uttered the memorable phrase, 'Will you take me in, please, mister?')

With the advent in the 1950s of more explicit films came the creation of the X certificate which, since X invariably meant sex, exhibitors were quick to exploit for their own uses; so much so that, by the end of the permissive 1960s, the number of films granted an X certificate was greater than all the A and U classifications combined.

All the while, local authorities had the power to overrule the censors' decision. From admittedly limited research, it seems that Harrow councillors have traditionally shown great reluctance to intervene. The release of *Crash* as recently as June 1997 provides a fairly typical example. This David Cronenburg adaptation of a J.G. Ballard novel, in which a married couple spice up their sex life by recreating famous car fatalities, gained such advance notoriety that a Liberal Democrat representative and former magistrate felt that the council should, at least, discuss the possibility of their imposing a ban on its showing locally (as had already happened in a few localities). However, his calls to action were ignored.

When the film duly opened at the Warner complex at the St George's Centre, he duly paid his money, only to walk out, creating a blaze of local press publicity about what he subsequently described as 'the most vile and pornographic film I have ever seen'.

Long before the X certificate was designed to exclude younger cinema patrons, horror movies such as Boris Karloff's *Frankenstein* had their own H certificate which served a similar purpose. *(Universal Films)*

By the early 1930s, when Charles Goddard wrote his critical report on films, Harrow had a notably handsome cinema in the Coliseum, Station Road (now the site of an Iceland supermarket).

In the event, it was the public, not the council, who decided the film's local fate. After one week with three performances a day, *Crash* was reduced to a single daily showing, late at night, the following week. By the third week, it had completely disappeared from local screens.

Coincidentally, the very same week, censorship of a far nastier kind was suspected in Edgware when the Belle-Vue cinema caught fire during a screening of a politically controversial Asian film called *Border*, whose Delhi performances had been cut short by an act of arson claiming the lives of some 60 cinemagoers. The police investigating officer thought the fire 'could possibly have been racially motivated' although the manager claimed a revenge attack by two youths banned from the cinema for illicit smoking. Whatever the motive of the attack, there were happily no casualties.

You may like to know that many European countries, including Denmark, Austria and Portugal, banished any kind of film censorship decades ago. One country is unique in never having exercised any form of control at any time. In case it ever crops up in a general knowledge quiz, I'll give you the somewhat surprising answer. It is Belgium, whose cinemas presumably never enjoyed – or endured – the patronage of Harrow's one-time Medical Officer.

Yew Walk

A poster from the year 1821 seeking a contractor 'to farm the poor of the parish', specifically, the Harrow Poor House inmates.

TO BE LET,
To FARM,
The POOR of the Parish of
HARROW ON THE HILL,
In the County of Middlesex,

Ten Miles from London, in a healthy Situation, with a good House and Garden, for One Year, to commence on the First Day of October, 1821, all the POOR in the House, and out of the House, and all Casualties. The Contractor is also to pay the Expenses of Removals, and every other Expense the Parish is liable to, except Repairs, Insurances of Buildings, County Rates, Expenses of Law Suits, and the Salary of the Apothecary and Surgeon.

Any further Information respecting the same will be given by Mr. WILLIAM WINKLEY, Vestry Clerk. Such Persons as are inclined to take the same, are to attend Personally, with their Proposals, at the Vestry Room of the said Parish, on Friday the 28th Day of September, 1821, at Five o'Clock in the Afternoon precisely, where the Inhabitants will attend to receive the Proposals.

A Character and Security will be required.

WINKLEY, Printer, St. John Street, Smithfield.

Yew Walk is not one of Harrow's most famous thoroughfares. It is, after all, a very short road and, compared with its medieval neighbours such as Crown Street and West Street, it is relatively new: in fact, the name does not even appear in local street directories until 1928 when the occupants of just four cottages were listed. Yet, in more recent times, this tranquil backwater has been at the centre of probably the biggest controversy that has ever divided Harrow Hill – the building of a theatre for Harrow School, now known (after its principal benefactor) as the Ryan Theatre.

It was, in effect, the site's total peacefulness that provoked the uproar in the first place since, for longer than most of us can remember, local folk have been used to taking themselves – and their dogs – down Yew Walk and on to the Church Fields, open space since at least the fourteenth century. As mentioned elsewhere, this whole area was once Roxeth Common, where the town's regular fairs and markets were traditionally held.

Probably nobody ever gave a thought to its ownership, assuming perhaps that, since the council cut the grass, it was most likely council property. In truth, as the town soon discovered, the land belonged to Harrow School which, for some decades, had permitted its use by the council on payment of a peppercorn rent. There was even a suggestion that it had come to the school as part of John Lyon's original endowment in the reign of the first Queen Elizabeth.

Nobody denied that the school deserved a proper theatre. But a lot of people were soon wondering if a more appropriate site could not be found, perhaps on the London side of Harrow Hill, where the school already had most of its sporting facilities. And this argument still held, even after the school had made it known that they would be willing to share the theatre with Harrow's townsfolk, who, notoriously, have lacked a theatre of their own since the closure of the Harrow Coliseum in Station Road in June 1956. Then, as far as residents were concerned, came an even bigger blow. As the theatre was to cost millions, part of its financing was to be raised by the building, as a strictly commercial venture, of a small estate of houses bordering Church Fields.

Although the plan included the retention of the original four cottages, it required the demolition of two others which had been added in the late 1920s by no less an architect than Sir Herbert Baker (whose more famous buildings included the Bank of England and Harrow School's War Memorial complex). These cottages were not notably distinguished in themselves but people were used to them; besides, they were highly appropriate to their setting – which was more than could be said for a new estate.

Amid scenes of increasing local acrimony, Harrow's councillors turned down the application. The school then appealed and, in the ultimate, an Inspector from the Department of the Environment found in their favour. By now the controversy, which had even divided staff and ex-pupils of the school itself, had reached the national press. 'Theatre plans create school for scandal', trumpeted a January 1990 *Observer* colour supplement, while, in an exchange of letters in *The Times*, the president of SAVE Britain's Heritage and other like-minded souls were 'appalled at the threatened vandalism imminently to be visited on its own surroundings by Harrow School'.

Yew Walk, as many remember it, before the controversial building of the late 1980s.

Locally, demonstrations were stepped up, major school events were picketed, and the contents of posters in windows in the area became so highly charged and inflammatory that the school cried 'libel'. But the protests were all in vain. The houses were finally built and the theatre duly opened with a gala performance in 1994, when the programme relied heavily on the work of distinguished Old Harrovians from Byron and Sheridan to Terence Rattigan and John Mortimer.

So what has happened some ten years on? The Ryan Theatre – plain on the outside but well-equipped within – is in almost constant use by the school and, well-screened by trees, is not nearly as obtrusive as so many feared (which is hardly true of the new houses, though they, too, are 'mellowing' with time).

Yew Walk in 1994, shortly after the building of the new estate.

Below: The plain exterior of the Ryan Theatre gives little hint of the pleasures within.

The real sadness is that, for obvious reasons, the theatre has never been licensed for public performance. However, on occasion, such as a St Mary's Music Festival and, more recently, the Salvation Army's 2003 Christmas concert, special licences have been granted and townsfolk have had the opportunity to see what they have been missing. Though I won't hold my breath, it would be nice to think that such events might provide a pointer to the theatre's ultimate role in the twenty-first century.

Before leaving Yew Walk, however, it's worth recalling a further point of interest for the local historian. The house still standing at its junction with West Street is genuinely one of the most interesting in Harrow. Now a school residence, it was built in about 1724 as the town's poor

This Grove Hill plaque pinpoints the location of the well named after Charles I. A persistent legend claims the monarch used it while fleeing for his life.

The former Poor House as it looked in about 1896 when its immediate neighbour was Woodbridge, the builder and plumber.

house (or workhouse). If that were not interest enough, it was constructed with materials taken from the 'house in the churchyard', which, as recorded in the very first chapter of this book, may well have been the original home of what ultimately became Harrow School.

As a workhouse, it could be occupied by as many as 50–60 poor souls during the winter when Harrow's status as an agricultural community meant a great deal of seasonal unemployment.

For all its strictness – there was partial segregation of the sexes by day and a total one at night, even for families – the poor house at least provided a roof over heads that would otherwise have been homeless, and what we would now call 'benefit fraud' was not unknown. In December 1841, the Vestry of St Mary's (who administered Poor Law relief) instructed parishioners in just what to do if they suspected anyone 'of imposing on the parish' – that is, unjustifiably claiming relief. Clearly and unambiguously, they were told to write down the offenders' details and to post them on the door of the parish church – an early example of what we would now call naming and shaming!

Zeppelins

By downing a German Zeppelin over British soil, William Leefe Robinson earned himself a Victoria Cross, and a secure place in local history.

No doubt about it – the very last word in *Harrow A to Z* has to be Zeppelin, not least because that most terrifying German war machine of the First World War was considered virtually invincible until a Stanmore pilot shot one down over Hertfordshire and became perhaps our most famous local VC.

Named after Ferdinand Von Zeppelin, the world's foremost designer of airships, the vast helium-filled dirigibles were originally used for naval reconnaissance patrols over the North Sea. However, the Germans were quick to realise their potential for something far more threatening – a weapon that could be used to drop bombs from a height too great for interception by defensive aircraft. Indeed, the first Zeppelin raids began within months of the outbreak of war, although London was not attacked until the following spring.

Even then, the good people of Harrow did not seem to consider themselves in danger. According to contemporary press accounts, Zeppelin activity over London was, at first, more a source of spectacle than of anxiety, being regularly watched by excited crowds gathered on such high vantage-points as Harrow Hill and Wealdstone railway bridge.

Though it still bore two wreaths in July 2004, William Leefe Robinson's grave in the cemetery across the road from All Saints, Harrow Weald, is probably little known to the majority of local residents.

An entry in October 1917 even refers, somewhat callously, to 'a wonderful air spectacle, the most wonderful that has ever been seen by residents'. Very properly, the local council took a more responsible attitude, circulating Harrow households with advice on extinguishing unnecessary lights and, in an intriguing foretaste of the Second World War's total blackout, suggesting that rooms should only be illuminated if their windows could be effectively screened.

By comparison, the nearby public house that bears his name is much visited. It even boasts a small exhibition in his memory.

Air raid precautions also included official Zeppelin-spotting from Harrow's highest view-points. In a now-it-can-be-told feature in January 1918, the *Harrow Observer* revealed that the first observation post – on top of Harrow School's high-standing Museum Schools in Football Lane – had been badly hampered by the lack of even such basic equipment as a telephone.

Fortunately, 'these deficiencies' were remedied by the Admiralty when the spotting was sensibly moved to the tower of St Mary's, the parish church on the very top of Harrow Hill. The move might well have been prompted by the fact that one General Ashmore, in charge of Air Defence, was the brother of Mrs Hayward Joyce, wife of the then Vicar of Harrow. But, whatever the reason, the all-important job of spotting was henceforth performed 'under conditions which carried with them a greater measure of success and utility'.

Though the accuracy of the bombs dropped by the Zeppelins was limited, their psychological impact was considerable because, for the very first time, they were able to bring the horrors of modern warfare to ordinary British doorsteps. So one can readily imagine the boost to public confidence when a 23-year-old flyer called William Leefe Robinson managed to shoot down a Zeppelin over Cuffley in Hertfordshire; a Zeppelin, incidentally, which had already been 'spotted' by the Harrow tower.

Robinson, whose wartime home was Lavender Cottage, Gordon Avenue, Stanmore, was promptly awarded the Victoria Cross, briefly becoming one of the most celebrated figures of the day. With very little training, he then became a fighter pilot but, on his very first flight in one of the new Bristol fighters, he was unlucky enough to be forced down on enemy soil – curiously enough, in the town of Douai, which, for some years past, has been Harrow's 'twin' in Europe.

Nor was this the end of his bad luck; Hauptmann Karl Niemeyer, the commandant of the prison camp to which he was sent, appears to have been a personal friend of the very man whose Zeppelin the British man had downed and ensured that Leefe Robinson suffered unusually severe privations. during his captivity. However, these were probably aggravated by his several attempts to escape. After one such bid for freedom, he was apparently punished by solitary confinement in a cubicle in which, it was said, he could neither sit nor stand comfortably – a truly agonising situation for someone around 6ft tall.

Harrow's first Zeppelin observation point was located on top of the multi-level block seen in the middle of this interwar picture. The building is now known as the Butler Museum Schools.

Not surprisingly, it was a much weakened and emaciated man who was finally repatriated to Stanmore on 14 December 1918. In this condition, he quickly fell victim to the influenza epidemic then raging through Europe and, despite the careful nursing of his sister and fiancée, he died on the last day of the year.

Both women were subsequently highly vocal in their condemnation of his treatment in enemy hands. His fiancée, Joan Whipple, told the *Harrow Observer* that the influenza was not the real cause of death. 'He was murdered by Niemeyer', she declared, 'who employed every instrument of cruelty against him'.

His sister, Baroness Heyking, added that Robinson himself had never spoken a word about his suffering – she claimed that the whole ghastly story had been revealed only while he was in an illness-induced delirium. Robinson was given a true hero's funeral before his burial in the new graveyard of All Saints, Harrow Weald. The ceremony included a flight of aircraft over the district during which a giant laurel wreath was dropped with such precision that mourners were able to retrieve it and place it on his coffin.

Today, of course, Leefe Robinson is probably best remembered by the well-known public house in Uxbridge Road, Harrow Weald. Not only does it bear his name, it also houses an exhibition which, though somewhat reduced in scale after a recent redecoration, is still a worthy recognition of a truly heroic achievement.

Harrow Weald, where Leefe Robinson is buried, was also the wartime site of a transit camp from which troops, such as these Seaforth Highlanders, were entrained directly to France and the trenches.

ACKNOWLEDGEMENTS

As I mentioned in my introduction, this book began life as a series of articles commissioned by the *Harrow Observer*, the borough's leading newspaper, which, after 150 years in print, is itself something of an historic institution!

It seems entirely appropriate, therefore, that they should so willingly have cooperated in the reappearance here of the original 26 articles in a new – and greatly extended – form. I am grateful, too, for permission to use many illustrations from the paper's archives.

Once again, I must also record my gratitude to Harrow's Local History Archivist Bob Thompson and his Civic Centre Library team for a host of irreplaceable benefits that range from the tireless checking of my text to the generous loan of many priceless prints and photographs now housed in the Borough's Local History Collection.